IT Auditor: Information Systems Audit Specialist Job Interview Bottom Line Questions and Answers: Your Basic Guide to Acing Any Information Technology Auditor Job Interview

Preface:

Sector: Information Technology

It's for the following Job interviews:
Information Technology Auditor
IT Risk and Compliance Specialist
IT Audit Support Specialist
The Strategist for IT Auditing
IT Audit Manager
IT Audit Strategist
IT Compliance
IT Auditing
IT Auditor

*****

Why this Book:

Why reinvent the wheel when you can use this book to convey powerful and useful technical information about an IT Auditor Job to the employer successfully.

This book tries to bring together the important IT Auditor Job interview information.

It has been well written to make it a very quick read for last-minute interview preparation in as low as 60 minutes.

Practicing with this interview questions and answers in the mirror will help with your replies to questions and pass with flying colors.

Also try to review this book an hour before the interview. It will help overcome nervousness and anxiety when interviewing. It covers technical, non-technical, HR and Personnel questions. You will learn to practice mock interviews for an IT Auditor Position.

Interview Questions and Suggested Answers related to the following and more:

IT risk analysis and remediation

Development and implementation of an effective IT audit plan

Information Technology and Information Systems risk assessment

Plan, coordinate, and perform the assessment of Information Systems internal controls

Utilize assessment to develop audit programs for testing controls

IT operational audits by verifying and examining records and procedures,

Internal controls and identifying potential improvements

Map processes to identify key risks and controls

Identifies and assesses key IT and data related risks and controls

Identify current and potential areas of risk

Perform non-SOX IT audits, and some SOX audits

Recommending improvements in current risk
management controls

Enterprise risk assessment and audit planning

Document and deliver audit reports and finding

Evaluate the design and effectiveness of automated
application controls

Identify root causes and develop formal
recommendations on improvements

INDEX

AS AN IT AUDITOR WHAT YOU RECOMMEND FOR APPLICATION TESTING

AS AN IT AUDITOR WHAT YOU RECOMMEND FOR REDUCING INFORMATION RISK?

AS AN IT AUDITOR WHAT YOU SUGGEST FOR DEBUGGING?

AS AN IT AUDITOR WHAT YOU RECOMMEND FOR OPERATING SYSTEM SECURITY

AS AN IT AUDITOR YOUR EXPERIENCE WITH VALIDATION SYSTEMS

AS AN IT AUDITOR WHICH ONLINE AUDITING TECHNIQUES YOU ARE FAMILIAR WITH?

AS AN IT AUDITOR WHAT FACTORS YOU CONSIDER FOR COMPUTER CENTER

AS AN IT AUDITOR WHAT RISKS YOU HAVE SEEN IN IT OUTSOURCING?

AS AN IT AUDITOR IDENTIFY THE FACTORS OF ITGC

AS AN IT AUDITOR HOW WILL YOU PERFORM RISK ASSESSMENT

AS AN IT AUDITOR WHAT RISK RESPONSES YOU WILL CONSIDER

AS AN IT AUDITOR IDENTIFY INTERNAL CONTROL IMPLICATIONS ASSOCIATED WITH AN IT ENVIRONMENT

AS AN IT AUDITOR DEFINE RECORD COUNT

AS AN IT AUDITOR DEFINE APPLICATION CONTROLS

AS AN IT AUDITOR IDENTIFY THE PURPOSE OF LIMIT
TESTS?

AS AN IT AUDITOR LIST THE THREE TYPES OF
CONTROL TOTALS

AS AN IT AUDITOR WHAT IS THE PURPOSE OF MISSING
DATA CHECKS?

AS AN IT AUDITOR DEFINE HASH TOTALS

AS AN IT AUDITOR DEFINE BATCH TOTALS

AS AN IT AUDITOR IDENTIFY THE OBJECTIVE OF INPUT
APPLICATION CONTROLS?

AS AN IT AUDITOR IDENTIFY MANAGEMENT
ASSERTIONS

AS AN IT AUDITOR IDENTIFY COSO INTERNAL
CONTROL FRAMEWORK

AS AN IT AUDITOR LIST PHASES OF AN IT AUDIT

AS AN IT AUDITOR LIST THE LIMITATIONS TO INTERNAL
CONTROLS

AS AN IT AUDITOR LIST ELEMENTS OF CONTROL
ENVIRONMENT

AS AN IT AUDITOR LIST ELEMENTS OF RISK
ASSESSMENT

AS AN IT AUDITOR IDENTIFY FACTORS OF AUDIT RISK FORMULA

AS AN IT AUDITOR WHAT TYPES OF INTERNAL CONTROLS YOU SUGGEST?

AS AN IT AUDITOR NAME SOME RISK RESPONSES

AS AN IT AUDITOR HOW WILL YOU PERFORM RISK ASSESSMENT

AS AN IT AUDITOR HOW WILL YOU FIX ERRORS AND FRAUD?

AS AN IT AUDITOR NAME DIFFERENT TYPES OF IT SECURITY ATTACKS?

AS AN IT AUDITOR WHICH CLOUD MODELS YOU HAVE WORKED WITH?

AS AN IT AUDITOR EXPLAIN TRANSACTION AUTHORIZATION

AS AN IT AUDITOR, IN TERMS OF SECURITY HOW EMPLOYEE FIRINGS SHOULD BE HANDLED?

AS AN IT AUDITOR WHY SHOULD YOU CONSIDER RENAMING THE ADMINISTRATOR ACCOUNT?

AS AN IT AUDITOR HOW WILL YOU TURN OFF UNUSED SERVICES ON UNIX SYSTEMS?

AS AN IT AUDITOR HOW WILL YOU PREVENT IP SPOOFING?

AS AN IT AUDITOR GIVE SOME NETWORK SECURITY ATTACKS EXAMPLES THAT YOU HAVE RESOLVED?

AS AN IT AUDITOR EXPLAIN THE NETWORK SECURITY METHODS THAT YOU HAVE USED?

AS AN IT AUDITOR EXPLAIN THE PRINCIPLE OF DEFAULT DENY?

AS AN IT AUDITOR EXPLAIN THE AREAS IMPACTED BY SOX

AS AN IT AUDITOR EXPLAIN THE PENALTIES FOR SOX NON-COMPLIANCE?

WHAT ACTIONS YOU AS AN IT AUDITOR CAN TAKE TO PROTECT COMPUTER SYSTEMS FOR CLIENT-SIDE SECURITY WHILE BROWSING THE WEB?

AS AN IT AUDITOR HOW WILL YOU SECURE THE ANONYMOUS ACCOUNT?

AS AN IT AUDITOR EXPLAIN WHY APPLICATION LAYER OF TCP/IP STACKS VERY WEAK LINK IN TERMS OF SECURITY?

AS AN IT AUDITOR WHICH SERVICES YOU SHOULD DISABLE ON A SYSTEM RUNNING WINDOWS OS?

EXPLAIN HOW WILL YOU MAKE A UNIX OR A LINUX SERVER SECURE?

AS AN IT SECURITY ADMIN WHAT ACTION YOU WILL TAKE TO FIX SHELLSHOCK VULNERABILITY?

HOW TO MAKE A WINDOWS SERVER SECURE?

EXPLAIN WHAT YOU WILL DO FOR SECURING WEB SERVERS?

WHAT NETWORK PERFORMANCE METRIC YOU WILL ANALYZE IN CASE OF HACK?

AS AN IT SECURITY ADMIN HOW WILL YOU SECURE A GLOBAL COMPANY?

EXPLAIN HOW YOU WILL SECURE ROUTER AND FIREWALL SYSTEMS?

WHAT YOU RECOMMEND FOR SECURING DATABASES?

EXPLAIN YOUR EXPERIENCE WITH SECURITY AUDIT?

NAME A FEW AUDIT TOOLS?

HOW TO GATHER AUDIT INFORMATION?

WHAT FACTORS DO YOU CONSIDER WHEN YOU DEVELOP A BUDGET?

EXPLAIN WHAT COMPONENTS YOU WILL USE IN NETWORK SECURITY SYSTEM?

WHY YOU NEED DIGITAL SIGNATURES?

LIST CRYPTOSYSTEMS TYPES?

EXPLAIN THE ADVANTAGES AND DISADVANTAGES OF PUBLIC-KEY CRYPTOGRAPHY?

DES ENCRYPTION LENGTH? WHY IT'S NOT USED NOW? WHATS THE ALTERNATIVE?

IN WINDOWS HOW IPSEC IS IMPLEMENTED?

WHAT IS A SECURITY POLICY? MECHANISM?

WHAT ACTION DEFINES SECURITY REQUIREMENTS?

WHAT MODES FILTERS CAN BE SET?

WHERE IPSEC FILTERS WORK?

IPSEC SERVICES?

DMZ CONTAINS WHAT COMPONENTS?

IS DMZ SECURE?

WHAT ARE AUTHENTICATION PROTOCOLS? NAME THEM?

WHAT IS SOCKS? BENEFITS OF SOCKS VERSION 5 PROXY SERVER?

WHAT IS AN IP DIRECTED BROADCAST? USE?

WHY TFTP IS INSECURE?

802.11B SUPPORTS WHAT ENCRYPTED STANDARD?

WHY YOU SHOULD RESTRICT ACCESS TO THE IIS ANONYMOUS ACCOUNT?

NAME A NETWORK SNIFFER

WHAT IS ICMP BOMBING?

WHAT YOU SUGGEST FOR PC FOR CLIENT-SIDE SECURITY THAT IS USED FOR BROWSING THE WEB?

WHICH TEST FILE CAN BE USED TO DETERMINE IF AN ANTI-VIRUS SCANNER IS WORKING?

HOW TO FIND IF YOUR COMPUTER HAS A MACRO VIRUS? HOW TO RESOLVE IT?

SECURITY TOKEN COMBINES WHICH TWO FACTORS?

HOW THE LANMAN CHALLENGE/RESPONSE AND NTLMV1 PROTOCOLS AUTHENTICATE USERS?

HOW A SCREENING ROUTER PROVIDES SECURITY?

WHAT ARE INFRASTRUCTURE ATTACKS?

HOW TO SECURE WIRELESS ROUTER?

WHAT IS CHARGEN?

WHAT IS A "BELT AND SUSPENDERS" APPROACH IN IT SECURITY?

WHAT ARE TWO USES OF THE TCP WRAPPERS PACKAGE?

WHAT IS NAT?

AS AN IT AUDITOR ACCOUNTING RECORDS

AS AN IT AUDITOR WHY YOU SUGGEST ACCESS CONTROL

AS AN IT AUDITOR WHY YOU SUGGEST INDEPENDENT VERIFICATION

AS AN IT AUDITOR WHY YOU SUGGEST APPLICATION CONTROLS

AS AN IT AUDITOR WHY YOU SUGGEST GENERAL CONTROLS

AS AN IT AUDITOR LIST DATA PROCESSING ELEMENTS

AS AN IT AUDITOR LIST INCOMPATIBLE IT FUNCTIONS

AS AN IT AUDITOR LIST DDP RISKS

AS AN IT AUDITOR LIST DDP ADVANTAGES

AS AN IT AUDITOR LIST DDP CONTROLS

AS AN IT AUDITOR LIST TYPES OF CLOUD COMPUTING

AS AN IT AUDITOR CLOUD COMPUTING IMPLEMENTATION ISSUES

AS AN IT AUDITOR LIST THE THREATS TO OPERATING SYSTEM INTEGRITY

AS AN IT AUDITOR WHICH ILLEGAL DENIAL-OF-SERVICE (DOS) ATTACKS YOU ARE FAMILIAR WITH?

AS AN IT AUDITOR LIST SOME COMPUTER-AIDED AUDIT TOOLS

GIVE SOME EXAMPLES OF UNNECESSARY SERVICES?

AS AN IT AUDITOR NAME THREE STEPS IN THE AUDIT PROCESS?

NAME THREE TYPES OF AUDIT

AS AN IT AUDITOR HOW WILL YOU TEST THE OPERATING EFFECTIVENESS OF THE CONTROLS?

AS AN IT AUDITOR WHAT ARE THE SOURCES OF IT RISK?

AS AN IT AUDITOR DEFINE INFORMATION ASSURANCE

AS AN IT AUDITOR IDENTIFY KEY COMPONENTS OF COSO FRAMEWORK

AS AN IT AUDITOR WHAT VALUES YOU CAN ADD TO ORGANIZATION

AS AN IT AUDITOR IDENTIFY FACTORS OF INTERNAL CONTROLS

AS AN IT AUDITOR IDENTIFY TYPES OF IT CONTROLS?

AS AN IT AUDITOR IDENTIFY FACTORS DEFINING A MATERIAL MISSTATEMENT

AS AN IT AUDITOR IDENTIFY FACTORS OF IT CONTROLS?

AS AN IT AUDITOR CAN YOU RECOGNIZE THE LAYERS OF *OSI MODEL*

AS AN IT AUDITOR CAN YOU IDENTIFY THE OBJECTIVES OF DISASTER RECOVERY PLANNING?

AS AN IT AUDITOR CAN YOU IDENTIFY CLOUD COMPUTING SERVICES

AS AN IT AUDITOR CAN YOU IDENTIFY THREATS OF CYBER SECURITY

AS AN IT AUDITOR CAN YOU IDENTIFY 2 SECURITY CONCEPTS AROUND DATA

AS AN IT AUDITOR WHAT IMPROVEMENTS YOU RECOMMEND IN PASSWORD CONTROLS?

AS AN IT AUDITOR CAN YOU IDENTIFY THE IT DUTIES THAT SHOULD BE SEGREGATED?

AS AN IT AUDITOR CAN YOU IDENTIFY AND ASSESS CONTROLS FOR HARDWARE AND SYSTEMS SOFTWARE.

AS AN IT AUDITOR CAN YOU IDENTIFY AND ASSESS CATEGORIES OF GENERAL CONTROLS.

AS AN IT AUDITOR CAN YOU IDENTIFY CONTROL TOTALS?

AS AN IT AUDITOR CAN YOU IDENTIFY LOGIC CHECKS?

AS AN IT AUDITOR CAN YOU IDENTIFY PHYSICAL CONTROLS

AS AN IT AUDITOR CAN YOU IDENTIFY IT CONTROLS

AS AN IT AUDITOR CAN YOU IDENTIFY THE FIVE ASSERTIONS

AS AN IT AUDITOR CAN YOU IDENTIFY THE *TYPES OF AUDIT RISK*

AS AN IT AUDITOR CAN YOU IDENTIFY WEB APPLICATION RISKS?

AS AN IT AUDITOR CAN YOU IDENTIFY COMPONENTS OF A COMPUTER-BASED IT AUDIT?

AS AN IT AUDITOR CAN YOU IDENTIFY 5 TECHNIQUES TO AUDIT COMPUTERIZED AIS- *ACCOUNTING INFORMATION SYSTEM*?

AS AN IT AUDITOR CAN YOU IDENTIFY SIGNIFICANT RISKS AROUND DATA SECURITY RELATED RISKS?

AS AN IT AUDITOR CAN YOU IDENTIFY SIGNIFICANT RISKS ABOUT GENERIC ACCOUNTS?

AS AN IT AUDITOR WHICH THREATS YOU WILL LOOK FOR IN CYBER SECURITY AUDIT

AS AN IT AUDITOR WHICH DATA SECURITY CONCEPTS YOU WILL VALIDATE?

AS AN IT AUDITOR WHICH PARTS OF THE FRAUD TRIANGLE YOU ARE FAMILIAR WITH?

AS AN IT AUDITOR IDENTIFY CONCEPTS OF IDM

AS AN IT AUDITOR WHAT YOU SUGGEST FOR PROVISIONING

AS AN IT AUDITOR WHAT ENFORCEMENT AND VERIFICATION OF IT CONTROLS YOU SUGGEST?

ENFORCEMENT OF (IDM)

AS AN IT AUDITOR IDENTIFY STANDARD STEPS IN THE IDM PROCESS?

AS AN IT AUDITOR IDENTIFY PCI REQUIREMENTS?

AS AN IT AUDITOR WHAT DATA PROTECTION TECHNIQUES YOU RECOMMEND?

AS AN IT AUDITOR IDENTIFY STEPS YOU WILL PERFORM IN AN INVESTIGATION FOR DATA?

AS AN IT AUDITOR IDENTIFY FACTORS IMPACTING IDM

AS AN IT AUDITOR IDENTIFY FACTORS IMPACTING PROVISIONING

AS AN IT AUDITOR IDENTIFY FACTORS IMPACTING ENFORCEMENT

AS AN IT AUDITOR IDENTIFY THE STEPS IN THE IDM PROCESS?

AS AN IT AUDITOR IDENTIFY THE METHODS FOR CONDUCTING A SECURITY CONTROL ASSESSMENT

AS AN IT AUDITOR IDENTIFY THE CLOSELY-RELATED AREAS OF COMPLIANCE?

AS AN IT AUDITOR IDENTIFY THE IMPACTS OF AUDITS AND ASSESSMENTS?

AS AN IT AUDITOR IDENTIFY THE IMPACTS OF NONCOMPLIANCE WITH REGULATORY STANDARDS?

AS AN IT AUDITOR IDENTIFY FACTORS IMPACTING HARDWARE AND SYSTEMS SOFTWARE

AS AN IT AUDITOR IDENTIFY CATEGORIES OF GENERAL CONTROLS

AS AN IT AUDITOR IDENTIFY FACTORS IMPACTING CONTROL TOTALS

AS AN IT AUDITOR IDENTIFY FACTORS IMPACTING GENERAL CONTROLS

AS AN IT AUDITOR LIST SOME INTERNAL CONTROL IMPLICATIONS ASSOCIATED WITH AN IT ENVIRONMENT.

AS AN IT AUDITOR LIST THE TYPES OF PHYSICAL SAFEGUARDS USED TO PROTECT THE DATA FILES?

AS AN IT AUDITOR WHICH IT DUTIES YOU WILL KEEP SEGREGATED

WHAT IS ICMP? WHAT IS ICMP BOMBING?

AS AN IT AUDITOR LIST SOME EXAMPLES OF LOGIC CHECKS

AS AN IT AUDITOR WHICH STEPS IN BCP CREATE AN EFFECTIVE BUSINESS CONTINUITY PLAN

AS AN IT AUDITOR WHAT FACTORS YOU CONSIDER OF A BCP?

AS AN IT AUDITOR WHAT FACTORS WILL YOU CONSIDER FOR DISASTER PLANNING?

AS AN IT AUDITOR HOW WILL YOU TACKLE FRAUD?

AS AN IT AUDITOR CAN YOU IDENTIFY APPLICATION CONTROL OBJECTIVES AND HOW TO ACHIEVE IT?

AS AN IT AUDITOR CAN YOU IDENTIFY IT AUDIT METHODOLOGIES

AS AN IT AUDITOR CAN YOU IDENTIFY COBIT - STRUCTURE

AS AN IT AUDITOR CAN YOU IDENTIFY COBIT - IT PROCESS MATRIX

AS AN IT AUDITOR CAN YOU IDENTIFY IT RESOURCES

AS AN IT AUDITOR CAN YOU IDENTIFY CONTROL CATEGORIES

AS AN IT AUDITOR CAN YOU IDENTIFY KEY CONTROLS

AS AN IT AUDITOR CAN YOU IDENTIFY BSI - SECURITY MEASURES

AS AN IT AUDITOR IDENTIFY AUDIT TRAILS RECORDS USEFUL FOR MAINTAINING SECURITY AND FOR RECOVERING LOST DATA

WHAT IS ITIL?

ITIL FRAMEWORK CONSISTS OF WHICH PROCESSES?

EXPLAIN ONE BENEFIT OF ITIL?

WHAT ARE THE BENEFITS OF IMPLEMENTING A SERVICE DESK?

WHAT PROCESSES ARE UTILIZED BY THE SERVICE DESK?

WHAT IS THE OBJECTIVE OF INCIDENT MANAGEMENT?

WHAT ARE THE BENEFITS OF AN INCIDENT MANAGEMENT PROCESS?

CAPACITY MANAGEMENT PROCESSES?

HOW WILL YOU TEST CONNECTIVITY BETWEEN WORKSTATIONS?

WHAT ARE THE MAIN COMPONENTS OF A COMPUTER?

HOW TO VIEW AND MANAGE HARDWARE DEVICES AND THEIR DEVICE DRIVERS IN WINDOWS?

LIST THREE DEVICES THAT ARE CONTAINED INSIDE THE COMPUTER CASE.

WHAT COMPUTER PARTS ARE INSIDE THE BOX?

HOW WILL YOU VERIFY CONFIGURATION INFORMATION ABOUT THE SYSTEM, SUCH AS DATE AND TIME, CPU, HARD DRIVES OR FLOPPY DRIVES?

HAVE YOU RECOVERED A SYSTEM BY RECOVERY CONSOLE?

WHEN HAVE YOU USED   SAFE MODE?

EXPLAIN SUBNET MASK?

HOW DO YOU KNOW IF THERE IS AN INTERMITTENT PROBLEM WITH THE ELECTRICAL SYSTEM?

HOW TO VERIFY HOW DEVICES ARE MANAGED?

EXPLAIN DRIVER SIGNING?

HOW WILL YOU EXAMINE AND CONFIGURE ALL THE HARDWARE AND DRIVERS INSTALLED ON A MACHINE?

EXPLAIN YOUR EXPERIENCE WITH RAID?

WHAT IS BIA? WHAT BUSINESS CONTINUITY COMPONENTS YOU WILL FOCUS ON?

WHY UNIX IS WIDELY USED?

ARE YOU FAMILIAR WITH UNIX COMMANDS?

WHAT IS A COMPUTER VIRUS?

WHAT ARE THE INFORMATION CLASSIFICATION LEVELS?

WHAT SECURITY MODES HAVE YOU WORKED ON?

WHAT IS CERTIFICATE AUTHORITY?

WHAT DOES A CERTIFICATE CONTAINS?

HOW TO CALCULATE SECURITY RISK?

WHAT ARE THE COMMON ISSUES WITH VULNERABILITY ASSESSMENT TOOLS?

WHAT ARE THE CLASSES OF ATTACKS AGAINST SANS?

WHAT ARE THE CLASSIFICATION CRITERIA FOR DATA SECURITY?

WHAT IS IANA?

EXPLAIN YOUR EXPERIENCE WITH NFS?

WHAT IS THE ROLE OF APPLICATION LAYER?

WHAT IS CRAMMING?

EXPLAIN RC4 WITH MD5?

EXAMPLES OF DENIAL OF SERVICE (DOS) ATTACKS?

WHAT IS CVE?

WHAT IS *SALAMI ATTACK?*

WHAT DOES MULTIPARTITE VIRUS MEAN?

WHAT IS SEPARATION OF DUTIES?

WHATS POLYMORPHIC VIRUS?

WHAT TYPES OF FIREWALLS YOU KNOW?

WHAT IS DAC - DISCRETIONARY ACCESS CONTROL?

WELL KNOWN PORTS?

EXPLAIN PING OF DEATH? HOW TO SEND IT?

HAVE YOU USED TRIPWIRE?

WHAT IS ROT13?

EXPLAIN SOURCE QUENCH?

EXPLAIN TROJAN HORSE?

EXPLAIN THE MAJOR DIFFERENCE(S) BETWEEN BLOCK AND STREAM CIPHERS?

WHAT IS SATAN?

WHAT ARE THE TYPES OF IT SECURITIES YOU HAVE EXPERIENCED WITH?

WHY CLIPPING LEVELS ARE USED?

HAVE YOU USED THE CROSSOVER ERROR RATE (CER)?

HAVE YOU WORKED WITH ONE TIME PASSWORDS – TOOLS?

EXPLAIN MASQUERADING?

EXPLAIN PDRR?

WHAT IS INFORMATION SECURITY AIC TRIAD?

WHATS YOUR EXPERIENCE WITH NONREPUDIATION?

WITH PRETTY GOOD PRIVACY (PGP) WHAT CAN BE ENCRYPTED?

WHAT IS AUDIT TRAIL?

WHAT ARE THE FOUR MAJOR COMPONENTS OF THE THREAT ASSESSMENT?

EXPLAIN SINGLE SIGN-ON (SSO)?

HAVE YOU USED SYMMETRIC KEY CRYPTOGRAPHY?

WHAT IS MOM AND HOW IT RELATES TO INSIDERS?

WHAT METHODS CAN BE USED TO PREVENT COLLUSION?

HOW MANY PHASES ARE IN SYSTEM LIFE CYCLE?

HOW YOU CALCULATE THE RISK?

WHAT IS RESIDUAL RISK?

EXPLAIN SECURITY THROUGH PENETRATION TESTING?

WHAT IS TCSEC SECURITY BOOK?

WHAT IS TCSEC MANDATORY SECURITY POLICY?

WHAT ARE TCSEC TWO TYPES OF ASSURANCES?

WHAT TCSEC FOUR DIVISIONS HAVE YOU WORKED ON?

WHAT IS A COVERT CHANNEL?

WHAT ARE THE TYPES OF COVERT CHANNELS YOU HAVE WORKED ON?

DEFINE THREAT?

NAME A FEW NETWORK THREATS?

WHAT IS CROSS SITE REQUEST FORGERY?

WHAT SOLUTION YOU PROPOSE FOR CSRF ATTACK?

WHAT PORT IS USED BY PING?

WHAT ARE THE MOST IMPORTANT ELEMENTS OF THE SECURITY LIFE CYCLE?

WHAT IS A WORLD WIDE NAME (WWN)?

HOW TO YOU KEEP UPDATED ON NETWORK SECURITY?

WHAT PROBLEM YOU FACE WITH CLOUD BASED SECURITY SOLUTIONS?

HOW WILL YOU FIND AND INFECTED MACHINE?

HOW WILL YOU DESIGN AN IT SECURITY SOLUTION FOR HIGH HTTP/HTTPS TRAFFIC?

WHAT IS FCAP (FIBRE CHANNEL AUTHENTICATION PROTOCOL)?

WHAT ARE THE CHAP SECURITY LEVELS?

FOR SAN STORAGE ARRAY SECURE ADMINISTRATION WHAT YOU RECOMMEND?

FOR SAN SECURITY EXPLAIN SAN ZONING?

WHAT ARE THE DIFFERENT ACCESS CONTROLS TYPES?

EXPLAIN DISCRETIONARY ACCESS CONTROL (DAC)?

WHAT IS THE LIMITATION OF DAC?

EXPLAIN YOUR EXPERIENCE WITH MAC?

EXPLAIN THE USE OF ACCESS CONTROL LIST?

IF RDP IS UTILIZED, HOW WILL YOU SECURE WINDOWS?

WHAT AUTHENTICATION PROTOCOL YOU WILL USE FOR WINDOWS?

HOW WILL YOU DISABLE UNWANTED SERVICES IN UNIX?

HOW WILL YOU DISABLE UNWANTED TCP APPLICATION?

WHEN AND HOW WILL YOU REMOVE SETUID BITS?

IN UNIX WHERE WILL YOU DISABLE UNWANTED PROCESSES?

EXPLAIN THE CHAP SECURITY?

WHAT IS USED BY A KERBEROS AUTHENTICATION PROCESS?

WHAT IS A SMURF ATTACK? HOW TO PREVENT IT?

EXPLAIN PHAGE VIRUSES?

EXPLAIN STATIC NAT? HOW TO SECURE IT?

EXPLAIN YOUR EXPERIENCE WITH DMZ?

WHAT IS DEFENSE IN DEPTH?

WHAT DIFFERENT TYPES OF FIREWALLS ARE THERE?

PROXY SERVERS OPERATE AT WHICH TCP/IP LAYER OF OSI?

WHAT IS THE BEST PRACTICE FOR PATCH FOR IT SECURITY?

HOW TO AVOID BREAK-INS? WHICH USER ACCOUNTS SHOULD BE REMOVED?

WHICH ORGANIZATIONS WORK TO SETTLE DOMAIN NAME DISPUTES?

WHAT IS SECURED LINUX?

WHAT ARE THREE FUNCTIONAL COMPONENTS OF RADIUS OR TACACS+?

WHAT IS MOST IMPORTANT IT SECURITY POLICY FOR FIREWALL RULES?

WHAT IS MOST PREVALENT VECTOR FOR MALWARE INFECTIONS? HOW TO PROTECT?

HOW TO PREVENT NEW VIRUS AND WORM OUTBREAKS?

EXPLAIN A PERIMETER-BASED SOLUTION THAT CAN BLOCK EMAIL THREATS INCLUDING SPAM, VIRUSES, AND WORMS?

HOW TO CHECK IF ANTI-VIRUS SCANNER IS WORKING?

WHAT IS MICROSOFT WORD'S MACRO VIRUS PROTECTION TOOL, AND HOW DO I ACTIVATE IT?

WHAT IS THE ADVANTAGE OF SECURITY TOKENS?

DESCRIBE NTLM? HOW IT AUTHENTICATES?

HOW SCREENING ROUTER WORKS?

CAN YOU PROPOSE A SOLUTION FOR A STATEFUL PACKET FILTERING?

WHAT IS REVERSE FIREWALL? HOW IT ENHANCES SECURITY?

HOW TO PROTECT PASSWORD TOKEN?

WHAT IS OTP SECURITY?

WHAT HAPPENS WHEN WHEN MULTIPLE ADMINISTRATORS SHARE ACCESS TO A SINGLE PRIVILEGED ACCOUNT?

IN A WINDOWS WEB SERVER, THAT HAS TWO NETWORK INTERFACES HOW PREVENT ROUTING BETWEEN THEM?

IS IT POSSIBLE TO RECOVER PASSWORDS VIA BRUTE FORCE PASSWORD ATTACKS?

WHAT IS THE MOST EFFICIENT FILTERING METHOD IN LEAST TIME?

WHEN ASSIGNING SYSTEM PRIVILEGES, WHICH CATEGORIZATION PROVIDES THE GREATEST

FLEXIBILITY FOR SECURITY ADMINISTRATION?

WHICH NETWORK PROTOCOL PROVIDES SYSTEM AVAILABILITY INFORMATION?

HOW TO PROTECT DATA THAT IS ACCESSED VIA PC DESKTOP?

WHAT IS NIDS?

IF A CRIME CONTAIN A DIGITAL SIGNATURE WHAT SHOULD BE DONE WITH THE COMPUTER THAT WAS HACKED?

IN COMPUTER FORENSICS WHICH DATA THEY ARE CONCERNED WITH?

WHAT IS A DIGITAL ID?

WHAT MAKE A DIGITAL ID?

WHAT IS PUBLIC KEY INFRASTRUCTURE (PKI)? GIVE AN EXAMPLE.

WHAT IS A HASH ALGORITHM? GIVE SOME EXAMPLES.

WHAT IS A MESSAGE DIGEST?

WHO IS RESPONSIBLE FOR INSTALLING THE SECURITY PATCH?

IT IS THE CUSTOMER'S RESPONSIBILITY TO INSTALL THE SECURITY PATCH.

WHAT KIND OF RIGHTS YOU WILL ALLOW FOR SERVER SERVICES OR ALL SERVICES?

WHAT DOES YOUR DIGITAL CERTIFICATE REPRESENTS? HOW TO PROTECT?

CERTIFICATES ARE AUTHENTICATED, ISSUED BY WHOM?

HOW TO VERIFY THE DIGITAL SIGNATURE OF THE ISSUING AUTHORITY?

WHEN AND WHY TO USE PROFESSIONAL ACCOUNTING AND AUDIT FIRMS?

AUDIT ACCURACY AND RELIABILITY OF CORPORATE CERTIFICATE AUTHORITY'S ISSUANCE POLICY.

HOW MANY WAYS AND A FIREWALL MANAGEMENT PROGRAM CAN BE CONFIGURED?

WHAT IS THE ONLY WAY TO GUARD AGAINST APPLICATION LAYER ATTACKS?

WHICH COMMAND WILL SHOW YOU WHICH PORTS ARE OPEN OR IN USE?

WHY SECURITY PATCHES SHOULD BE INSTALLED IMMEDIATELY?

WHAT IS IKE?

WHAT ARE SYMMETRIC KEY CRYPTOGRAPHIC ALGORITHMS? WHY YOU NEED THEM?

WHAT IS THE USE OF MESSAGE DIGEST FUNCTIONS? WHICH ARE COMMONLY USED?

FROM WHERE THE ENCRYPTION ALGORITHM IS INHERITED? WHAT ARE THE CLASSES?

WHAT IS TRANSPORT AGENT?

HOW TO PREVENT A SINGLE POINT OF FAILURE IN SECURITY MECHANISMS?

HOW CAN YOU IMPLEMENT SYNERGISTIC SECURITY?

WHAT IS AN ACCEPTABLE USE POLICY?

EXPLAIN POLP?

WHAT YOU SHOULD DO IF YOU RECEIVED A VIRUS WARNING FROM YOUR FRIEND?

WHAT IS STO?

WHAT ARE RECOMMENDED ED SYNERGISTIC CONTROLS AT THE DESKTOP-LEVEL?

WHY YOU NEED ACCESS LISTS?

WHAT IS THE USE OF DIGITAL SIGNATURES?

WHAT PROBLEMS HAVE YOU NOTICED WITH FTP?

WHAT KIND OF SECURITY ISSUE YOU HAVE DEALT WITH IN NIS?

WHAT IS DNS CACHE POISONING?

WHAT IS WEBSITE CRAWLING? IS IT AND AN ATTACK?

WHY TO PROTECT YOUR WEBSITE FROM A CRAWLER?

WEBSITE CRAWLING ROBOTS DRASTICALLY EATS UP A WEBSITE'S BANDWIDTH UNNECESSARILY.

FOR WHAT IS IMAP USED?

WHAT IS FTP, IN TERMS OF SECURITY WHAT MAKES IT DIFFICULT TO CONTROL THE FILE TRANSFER PROTOCOL (FTP) VIA A FIREWALL RULE SET OR PACKET FILTER?

EXPLAIN YOUR EXPERIENCE WITH DNS, AND WHAT YOU DID TO MAKE IT SECURE?

HOW DOES DNSSEC PROVIDE GREATER SECURITY?

WHAT ARE THE TASKS ASSOCIATED WITH DNSSEC?

WHAT IS SMTP, WHICH PORT IT RUNS? EXPLAIN HOW TO MAKE IT SECURE?

WHEN TO USE TRIPWIRE?

YOU HAVE TO SAVE STORAGE AND BACKUP DATA WITH SECURITY, HOW YOU CAN DO IT?

WHAT IS A BONNET?

WHAT SECURITY FEATURES YOU SHOULD LOOK FOR IN SOFTWARE?

TELL US WHAT YOU KNOW ABOUT WEB INTRUSION DETECTION SYSTEM?

WHAT IS CROSS SITE SCRIPTING?

CAN HTTP HANDLE STATE?

WHAT KEY WILL YOU USE FOR ENCRYPTION AND WHICH ONE WILL YOU USE FOR SIGNING?

WHAT TYPE OF HOME NETWORK DO YOU USE?

WHAT ARE TCP INFRASTRUCTURE ATTACKS?

HOW TO SECURE A ROUTER?

WHAT PORTS ARE ECHO SERVICE AND CHARGEN?

WHAT IS THE PURPOSE OF CHARGEN (PORT 19)?

EXPLAIN TCP AND UDP SMALL SERVERS?

EXPLAIN UDP SMALL SERVERS?

WHAT IS SOCKS?

WHAT IS BELT AND SUSPENDERS?

WHAT ARE TWO USES OF THE TCP WRAPPERS PACKAGE?

WHAT IS NETWORK ADDRESS TRANSLATION (NAT)? WHEN TO USE IT?

WHAT IS DEFENSE IN DEPTH?

PROXY SERVERS OPERATE AT WHICH TCP/IP LAYER?

WHAT IS THE BEST PRACTICE FOR PACHING OS?

HOW TO TO AVOID SECURITY BREAK-INS ON USER ACCOUNTS ON INTERNET SERVERS?

HOW TO MANAGE SOFTWARE LICENSES?

WHICH ORGANIZATIONS WORK TO SETTLE DOMAIN NAME DISPUTES?

WHAT IS SELINUX?

WHY RADIUS IS USED?

WHAT IS THE BEST PRACTICE FOR MAKING CHANGES TO THE FIREWALL CONFIGURATION?

WHAT SECURITY RULE YOU HAVE FOR DIAL-IN MODEMS?

WHICH FILE TYPE YOU SHOULD NEVER OPEN?

WHICH INTERNATIONAL ORGANIZATION PROVIDES COPYRIGHT LAW?

WHATS YOUR VIEW ABOUT REUSABLE PASSWORD?

WHAT IS HASH?

NAME 2 MOST USED CRYPTOGRAPHIC HASH FUNCTIONS?

HAVE YOU USED ESP? WHY?

HOW TO DEFENDING AN ENTERPRISE NETWORK AGAINST INTERNAL THREATS?

CAN YOU PROPOSE SOLUTIONS THAT OFFER FULL PROTECTION IN DEFENDING AN ENTERPRISE NETWORK AGAINST EXTERNAL THREATS?

WHAT IS ONE USE OF FIREWALLS?

WHATS YOUR RECOMMENDATION ON FIREWALLS?

WHAT IS THE MOST COMMON FORM OF SECURITY VULNERABILITY?

BUFFER OVERFLOWS

WHAT DO DIGITAL CERTIFICATES USED TO EXCHANGE TO GET PUBLIC KEY?

IN WHICH X.509 CERTIFICATE HANDLING AND PROCESSING DEFINED?

NAME TWO METHODS USED BY ENTRUST/PKI TO EXTEND TRUST BETWEEN CERTIFICATION

AUTHORITIES (CAS)?

WHICH IS A STEP IN SYSTEM HARDENING?

WHAT IS ONE OF THE MOST COMMON AVENUES OF ATTACK USED FOR SYSTEM BREAK-INS?

WHAT IS A DENIAL-OF-SERVICE (DOS) ATTACK?

WHAT IS GRAYWARE?

WHAT IS THE PRIMARY MECHANISM FOR A MALICIOUS CODE TO ENTER A DESKTOP?

WHAT IS A DATA WAREHOUSE?

WHAT IS THE DEFAULT CIPHER FOR THE IPSEC?

WHAT IS THE DIFFERENCE BETWEEN CLEARING AND PURGING INFORMATION?

NAME ENCRYPTION SOFTWARE IMPLEMENTATIONS?

WHAT PROBLEMS YOU HAVE SEEN IN KERBEROS IMPLEMENTATION?

SECURE SOCKET LAYER WORKS AT WHICH TCP/IP LAYER?

WHEN IS DES REQUIRED?

WHEN VPNS SHOULD BE USED?

WHAT STEPS YOU WILL TAKE TO SECURE YOUR WIRELESS LAN?

WHAT HAPPENS IN SOCIAL ENGINEERING ATTACK?

HOW TO AVOID SOCIAL ENGINEERING AND PHISHING ATTACKS?

WHAT IS COLD SPARE IN DISASTER RECOVERY?

WHAT ARE HONEY POTS?

HOW TO PROVIDE SECURITY BY HOST-BASED INTRUSION PREVENTION SYSTEMS (HIPSS)?

HOW INTRUSION DETECTION SYSTEMS ARE CLASSIFIED? TYPES?

HOW LFM PROVIDES SECURITY?

LOG FILE MONITORS (LFM)

HOW TO FIND THE CHAIN OF CUSTODY FOR COMPUTER RELATED ISSUES?

WHAT A SECURITY INCIDENT RESPONSE PROCEDURE DOCUMENT CONTAINS?

WHAT IS PENETRATION TESTING?

WHY AND HOW TO PERFORM THE PENETRATION TESTING FOR WEB APPLICATIONS?

WHAT TO MONITOR IN EMPLOYEE INTERNET USAGE?

HOW MANY BACKUPS NEEDED FOR BEST PROTECTION AGAINST DATA LOSS?

WHAT ARE THE SECURITY STANDARDS FOR MERCHANTS ACCEPTING CREDIT CARDS?

NAME A FEW SECURITY REQUIREMENTS FOR CLOUD?

NAME A FEW SECURITY TECHNOLOGIES THAT CAN BE USED FOR CLOUD COMPUTING ENVIRONMENT?

WHAT IS PCI DSS?

WHICH ARE POPULAR EMAIL PORTS?

EXPLAIN YOUR EXPERIENCE WITH SSL? WHAT ARE SECURITY LEVELS?

EXPLAIN THE USE OF TCP WRAPPERS?

EXPLAIN YOUR EXPERIENCE WITH THE RPC MAPPER? WHAT KIND OF ATTACK HAPPENS ON RPC?

EXPLAIN YOUR EXPERIENCE WITH JAVA SECURITY ISSUES?

HOW TO AVOID BRUTE –FORCE ATTACKS?

EXPLAIN YOUR EXPERIENCE WITH APACHE VULNERABILITIES?

EXPLAIN OPENSSH SIGNAL HANDLING VULNERABILITY?

WHAT IS ZERO-DAY ATTACKS?

IN TERMS OF SECURITY WILL YOU USE SWITCH OR A HUB?

WHAT IS FILTERING?

HOW DOES A PACKET FILTER WORK?

NAME THE TYPES OF FILTER TECHNIQUES?

HOW TO MAKE A SECURE WEB SERVER?

HOW TO CALCULATE RISK RELATED TO IT SECURITY?

EXPLAIN PORT SCAN ATTACK?

WHAT IS POINT-TO-POINT TUNNELING PROTOCOL (PPTP)? WHY NOT USE PPTP?

WHAT IS THE DEFAULT PORT FOR HTTP SERVICE?

EXPLAIN YOUR EXPERIENCE WITH SMB? IS SMB SECURE?

IS IT POSSIBLE TO CRACK PASSWORD THAT IS ENCRYPTED?

WHAT IS SPOOFING?

WHAT IS THE MOTIVE BEHIND THE DENIAL OF SERVICE ATTACK?

WHICH PORTS USED BY WINDOWS ARE MOST VULNERABLE?

WHICH PORTS NETBIOS USES OVER TCP?

EXPLAIN YOUR EXPERIENCE WITH A PERSONAL FIREWALL?

WHAT YOU LOOK FOR IN A FIREWALL?

WHAT METHOD MOST FIREWALLS CAN USE TO INFORM AN ADMINISTRATOR WHAT IS GOING ON?

EXPLAIN YOUR EXPERIENCE WITH DEMILITARIZED ZONE (DMZ) FOR SECURITY?

AS AN IT AUDITOR WHAT YOU KNOW ABOUT IOPS?

AS AN IT AUDITOR WHAT YOU KNOW ABOUT WWN

AS AN IT AUDITOR WHAT YOU KNOW ABOUT FIBRE CHANNEL LAYERS

AS AN IT AUDITOR WHAT YOU KNOW ABOUT EUI - EXTENDED UNIQUE IDENTIFIER FORMAT THE IEEE DEFINED 64-BIT EXTENDED UNIQUE IDENTIFIER (EUI-64) IS A CONCATENATION OF A 24-BIT ORGANIZATIONALLY UNIQUE IDENTIFIER (OUI) VALUE ADMINISTERED BY THE IEEE REGISTRATION AUTHORITY AND A 40-BIT EXTENSION IDENTIFIER ASSIGNED BY THE ORGANIZATION WITH THAT OUI ASSIGNMENT.

AS AN IT AUDITOR WHAT YOU KNOW ABOUT SCSI STANDARDS

AS AN IT AUDITOR WHAT YOU KNOW ABOUT SHARE RECOVERY TIERS

AS AN IT AUDITOR WHAT YOU KNOW ABOUT RAID SPECIFICATIONS

AS AN IT AUDITOR WHAT YOU KNOW ABOUT LUN ID

AS AN IT AUDITOR WHAT YOU KNOW ABOUT HDD RELIABILITY

AS AN IT AUDITOR WHAT YOU KNOW ABOUT
SUPPORTED DISTANCES OF THE VARIOUS 62.5-MICRON
CABLES

AS AN IT AUDITOR WHAT YOU KNOW ABOUT BUFFER
TO BUFFER CREDITS FOR LONG DISTANCE

AS AN IT AUDITOR WHAT YOU KNOW ABOUT
AVAILABILITY

AS AN IT AUDITOR WHAT YOU KNOW ABOUT LATENCY
AND RPM

AS AN IT AUDITOR WHAT YOU KNOW ABOUT SAS

AS AN IT AUDITOR WHAT YOU KNOW ABOUT RETURN
ON INVESTMENT (ROI)

AS AN IT AUDITOR WHAT YOU KNOW ABOUT
RECOVERY

AS AN IT AUDITOR WHAT YOU KNOW ABOUT MODE
CONDITIONING FIBER OPTIC CABLE

AS AN IT AUDITOR WHAT YOU KNOW ABOUT DATA-AT-
REST ENCRYPTION

AS AN IT AUDITOR WHAT YOU KNOW ABOUT LINUX
OPERATING SYSTEMS COMMANDS?

AS AN IT AUDITOR WHAT YOU KNOW ABOUT WI-FI
SECURITY

AS AN IT AUDITOR WHAT YOU KNOW ABOUT BOTNET

AS AN IT AUDITOR WHAT YOU KNOW ABOUT MALWARE

AS AN IT AUDITOR WHAT YOU KNOW ABOUT IP
ADDRESS CLASSES

AS AN IT AUDITOR WHAT YOU KNOW ABOUT MAC
ADDRESS FORMAT

AS AN IT AUDITOR WHAT YOU KNOW ABOUT
MULTICAST

AS AN IT AUDITOR WHAT YOU KNOW ABOUT UNICAST

AS AN IT AUDITOR WHAT YOU KNOW ABOUT
BROADCAST

AS AN IT AUDITOR WHAT YOU KNOW ABOUT IPV6

AS AN IT AUDITOR WHAT YOU KNOW ABOUT LOOP
BACK ADDRESS

AS AN IT AUDITOR WHAT YOU KNOW ABOUT THE
STANDARD PORTS

AS AN IT AUDITOR WHAT YOU KNOW ABOUT TRACERT

AS AN IT AUDITOR WHAT YOU KNOW ABOUT DSL

BOTTOM LINE JOB INTERVIEW?

INTERVIEW QUESTION?

WHAT ARE YOUR GREATEST STRENGTHS?

WHAT ARE YOUR GREATEST WEAKNESSES?

HAD YOU FAILED TO DO ANY WORK AND REGRET?

WHERE DO YOU SEE YOURSELF FIVE YEARS FROM NOW?

HOW WILL YOU ACHIEVE YOUR GOALS?

WHY ARE YOU LEAVING YOUR CURRENT POSITION?

WHY ARE YOU LOOKING FOR A NEW JOB?

WHY SHOULD I HIRE YOU?

AREN'T YOU OVERQUALIFIED FOR THIS POSITION?

DESCRIBE A TYPICAL WORK WEEK?

ARE YOU WILLING TO TRAVEL?

DESCRIBE THE PACE AT WHICH YOU WORK?

HOW DID YOU HANDLE CHALLENGES?

HOW DO YOU HANDLE PRESSURE? STRESSFUL SITUATIONS?

HOW MANY HOURS DO YOU WORK?

WHY ARE YOU THE BEST PERSON FOR THE JOB?

WHAT ARE YOU LOOKING FOR IN A POSITION?

WHAT DO YOU KNOW ABOUT OUR ORGANIZATION?

WHAT ARE YOUR SHORT TERM GOALS?

WHAT SALARY ARE YOU LOOKING FOR?

TELL ME MORE ABOUT YOURSELF.

WHY DID YOU LEAVE YOUR PREVIOUS JOB?

WHAT RELEVANT EXPERIENCE DO YOU HAVE?

IF YOUR PREVIOUS CO-WORKERS WERE HERE, WHAT WOULD THEY SAY ABOUT YOU?

WHERE ELSE HAVE YOU APPLIED?

WHAT MOTIVATES YOU TO DO A GOOD JOB?

ARE YOU GOOD AT WORKING IN A TEAM?

HAS ANYTHING EVER IRRITATED YOU ABOUT PEOPLE YOU'VE WORKED WITH?

IS THERE ANYONE YOU JUST COULD NOT WORK WITH?

TELL ME ABOUT ANY ISSUES YOU'VE HAD WITH A PREVIOUS BOSS.

DO YOU HAVE ANY QUESTIONS?

WHY DID YOU CHOOSE THIS CAREER?

WHAT DID YOU LEARN FROM YOUR LAST JOB EXPERIENCE?

HOW DO YOU KEEP CURRENT AND INFORMED ABOUT YOUR JOB AND THE INDUSTRIES THAT YOU HAVE WORKED IN?

TELL ME ABOUT A TIME WHEN YOU HAD TO PLAN AND COORDINATE A PROJECT FROM START TO FINISH?

WHAT KINDS OF PEOPLE DO YOU HAVE DIFFICULTIES WORKING WITH?

WHAT DO YOU WANT TO BE IN 5 YEARS?

EXPLAIN AN IDEAL CAREER FOR YOU?

WHAT ARE YOUR JOB RESPONSIBILITIES?

WHAT IS YOUR DREAM JOB?

WHAT SKILLS YOU HAVE?

WHAT SETS YOU APART?

IF THE PROJECT NOT GONE AS PLANNED WHAT ACTION YOU WILL TAKE?

WHAT YOU DO IF YOU ARE UNABLE TO MEET DEADLINES?

INTERPERSONAL SKILL?

IMPROVE?

WHAT DO YOU FEEL HAS BEEN YOUR GREATEST WORK-RELATED ACCOMPLISHMENT?

HAVE YOU EVER HAD TO DISCIPLINE A PROBLEM EMPLOYEE? IF SO, HOW DID YOU HANDLE IT?

WHY DO YOU WANT THIS POSITION?

WHY ARE YOU THE BEST PERSON FOR THIS JOB?

WHAT ABOUT TECHNICAL WRITING?

HOW VERSATILE YOU ARE? CAN YOU DO OTHER WORKS?

HOW DO YOU MANAGE TIME?

HOW DO YOU HANDLE CONFLICTS?

WHAT KIND OF SUPERVISORY SKILLS YOU HAVE?

ANY BAD SITUATION YOU COULD NOT SOLVE?

ANYTHING ELSE YOU WANT TO SAY?

ABOUT THE AUTHOR:

Bottom Line Job interview?

**Bottom line: You will learn to answer any questions in such a way that
You match your qualifications to the job requirements.**

As an IT Auditor explain why audits are needed?

❖ **Reducing information risk**
❖ **Reducing cost of capital**
❖ **Compliance with the laws and regulations**
❖ **To ensure that data is accurate, unaltered, and offers a true representation of the company's financial position.**

As an IT Auditor what internal and operational CONTROLS improvements you advise?

❖ ***IMPLEMENT* Parity checking: checks for completeness of data**
❖ **Implement Echo check: to check the reliability of computer hardware**

- ❖ Implement Diagnostic routines: to locate a computer malfunction
- ❖ Implement Boundary protection: the monitoring and control of communications

As an IT Auditor can you suggest categories of general controls applied to every system?

- ❖ Organization and operation
- ❖ Systems development and documentation
- ❖ Hardware and systems software
- ❖ Access controls security features
- ❖ Data and procedures

As an IT Auditor what improvements in Segregation of Duties you suggest?

I will implement Segregation of Duties (SOD) for sustainable risk management and internal controls for a business

I will select the combination of duties which would result in the least risk

- ❖ Systems analyst
- ❖ Programmer
- ❖ Operator
- ❖ Librarian
- ❖ Security

As an IT Auditor what you recommend for validity checks?

To determine whether the data under review is recognized as a legitimate possibility

- ❖ Transaction Validation
- ❖ Sequence Check
- ❖ Range Check
- ❖ Validity Check
- ❖ Reasonableness Check
- ❖ Existence Check
- ❖ Key Verification
- ❖ Check Digit
- ❖ Completeness Check
- ❖ Duplicate Check
- ❖ Logical Relation Check

As an IT Auditor what types of IT Controls you suggest?

- ❖ General Controls
- ❖ Application Controls

As an IT Auditor what types of Physical Controls you suggest?

- ❖ Independent Verification
- ❖ Transaction Authorization
- ❖ Segregation of Duties
- ❖ Supervision
- ❖ Accounting Records
- ❖ Access Control

As an IT Auditor explain what causes Information Risk?

- ❖ Remoteness of information
- ❖ Risk-based decision making
- ❖ Bias and Motives of the Provider
- ❖ Complex exchange transactions
- ❖ Transactions are increasingly complex

As an IT Auditor what you recommend for Application testing

- ❖ Test Data: Test transactions go through real programs
- ❖ Integrated Testing Facilities: Creates test transactions to include with live data
- ❖ Transaction Selection Programs: Screen and selects transaction input to regular production cycle
- ❖ Embedded Audit Data: Statistically-distributed input transactions

As an IT Auditor what you recommend for reducing information risk?

- ❖ Verification, Validation, and Evaluation of information by User
- ❖ Sharing of information risk with management by user
- ❖ Hold management responsible if inaccurate information is provided
- ❖ Engage External auditors to provide reliable financial statements

As an IT Auditor what you suggest for Debugging?

- ❖ Mapping: Identifies specific program's logic that have not been tested
- ❖ Tracing and tagging: Trace shows trail of instructions executed
- ❖ Snapshot: Records flow of designated transactions through logic paths

As an IT Auditor what you recommend for Operating System Security

❖ Log-on procedure: Secure Log-on Procedure
❖ Access token: token includes the identity and privileges of the user account
❖ Access control list: list of access control entries
❖ Discretionary access privileges: the owner determines object access privileges

As an IT Auditor your experience with Validation Systems

❖ Base-case system evaluation: Uses test data for testing programs and verifies correct system operations before accepting
❖ Parallel Simulation: Uses programs that simulate application program logic
❖ Parallel Operation: Compares new and old production data processing systems and compares results

As an IT Auditor which Online Auditing Techniques you are familiar with?

❖ **Systems Control Audit Review File and Embedded Audit Modules**
❖ **Snapshots: Pictures of the processes' path**
❖ **Audit Hooks: Embedding hooks in applications**
❖ **Integrated Test Facility (ITF): Dummy entries are set up and include auditor's production file**
❖ **Continuous & Intermittent Simulation (CIS): Simulates the instructions executed of the application**

As an IT Auditor what factors you consider for Computer Center

❖ **Physical location**
❖ **Construction**
❖ **Access**
❖ **Air-conditioning**

- ❖ Fire suppression
- ❖ Fault tolerance

As an IT Auditor what risks you have seen in IT Outsourcing?

- ❖ Failure to perform: failure to perform in an agreement
- ❖ Vendor exploitation: exploiting a country's comparative advantage through outsourcing.
- ❖ Outsourcing costs exceed benefits: There are hidden costs involved
- ❖ Reduced security: Risk of exposing confidential data
- ❖ Loss of strategic advantage: competition

As an IT Auditor identify the factors of ITGC

IT general controls (ITGC) are controls that apply to all systems components,
Processes and data for a given organization or information technology (IT) environment
Controls that have pervasive effects on all the specific computer processing applications:

- ❖ Logical access controls over infrastructure, applications, and data
- ❖ System development life cycle controls
- ❖ Program change management controls
- ❖ Data center physical security controls
- ❖ System and data backup and recovery controls
- ❖ Computer operation controls

As an IT Auditor how will you perform Risk Assessment

- ❖ I will define risk
- ❖ I will determine which controls mitigate this risk
- ❖ I will assess the design of controls

As an IT Auditor what Risk responses you will consider

Strategy for negative risk

- ❖ Avoid :*REDUCE* the *RISK*

- ❖ Mitigate: identify and mitigate risks
- ❖ Accept: *ACCEPTED AUDITING* standards
- ❖ Transfer: *TRANSFER AUDITS*

As an IT Auditor Identify internal control implications associated with an IT environment

- ❖ Segregation of duties may be undermined
- ❖ Audit trail may be lacking
- ❖ Computer processing is uniform

As an IT Auditor define record count

- ❖ A counting mechanism in an IT system that keeps track of the number of records
- ❖ Processed to determine that the appropriate number was accounted for

As an IT Auditor define application controls

Information processing controls that applies to the processing of specific computer applications.
Purpose of output application controls:

- ❖ To ensure the output data is accurate and as authorized
- ❖ Purpose of processing application controls
- ❖ To ensure the processing of data is accurate and as authorized

As an IT Auditor identify the purpose of limit tests?

To determine whether the data under review are all within some predetermined range

As an IT Auditor List the three types of control totals

- ❖ Batch totals
- ❖ Hash totals
- ❖ Record count

As an IT Auditor what is the purpose of missing data checks?

To determine whether there are any omissions from fields in which data should have been present

As an IT Auditor define hash totals

- ❖ An arbitrary total that has no meaningful interpretation outside the context in which it was created

❖ It is used only to validate the integrity of the data being examined

As an IT Auditor Define batch totals

The sum of a particular field in a collection of items used as a control total to ensure that all data has been entered into a system

As an IT Auditor identify the objective of input application controls?

To ensure that the input of data is accurate and as authorized
- ❖ Data edits
- ❖ Separation of business functions
- ❖ Balancing of processing totals
- ❖ Transaction logging
- ❖ Error reporting

As an IT Auditor Identify Management Assertions

- ❖ Existence/Occurrence
- ❖ Completeness
- ❖ Rights and Obligations
- ❖ Valuation
- ❖ Presentation and Disclosure

As an IT Auditor Identify COSO Internal Control Framework

- ❖ Control Environment
- ❖ Risk Assessment
- ❖ Information and Communication
- ❖ Monitoring
- ❖ Control Activities

As an IT Auditor list Phases of an IT Audit

- ❖ Audit Planning
- ❖ Test of Controls
- ❖ Substantive Testing

As an IT Auditor list the Limitations to Internal Controls

- ❖ Possibility of error
- ❖ Circumvention
- ❖ Management override
- ❖ Changing conditions
- ❖ Collusion

As an IT Auditor list Elements of Control Environment

- ❖ Integrity and ethics of management
- ❖ Structure of organization

- ❖ Participation of BOD and audit committee
- ❖ Management philosophy and operating style
- ❖ Procedures for delegating responsibility and authority
- ❖ Management's methods of assessing performance
- ❖ External influences
- I. Organization's policies and practices for HR

As an IT Auditor list elements of risk assessment

- ❖ Changes in operating environment that creates new pressures
- ❖ New personnel with inadequate understanding of IC
- ❖ New systems that affect transaction processing
- ❖ Significant or rapid growth that strain IC
- ❖ Implementation of new tech
- ❖ Introduction of new product line
- ❖ Organizational restructuring
- ❖ Entering foreign markets
- ❖ Adoption of new accounting principles

As an IT Auditor Identify factors of Audit risk formula

- ❖ AR = IR x CR x DR
- ❖ This risk is composed of inherent risk (IR), control risk (CR) and detection risk (DR), and can be calculated thus: AR = IR × CR × DR.

As an IT Auditor what types of Internal Controls you suggest?

- ❖ Soft: intangible controls like morale
- ❖ Hard: explicit controls
- ❖ Preventative: to keep errors or irregularities from occurring
- ❖ Monitoring: assessment of internal control performance

As an IT Auditor name some risk responses

- ❖ Avoid

- ❖ Mitigate
- ❖ Accept
- ❖ Transfer

As an IT Auditor how will you perform Risk Assessment

- ❖ *I WILL DEFINE RISK*
- ❖ *I WILL DETERMINE WHICH CONTROLS MITIGATE THIS RISK*
- ❖ *I WILL ASSESS THE DESIGN OF CONTROLS*

As an IT Auditor how will you fix errors and fraud?

- ❖ I will Implement and strengthen physical controls
- ❖ I will Develop Preventive and Detective Internal Controls
- ❖ To prevent errors, inaccuracy or fraud before it occurs
- ❖ I will implement an effective fraud awareness program

As an IT Auditor name different types of IT Security attacks?

- ❖ Identity interception
- ❖ Masquerade
- ❖ Replay attack
- ❖ Data interception
- ❖ Manipulation
- ❖ Repudiation
- ❖ Macro viruses
- ❖ Denial of service
- ❖ Malicious mobile code
- ❖ Misuse of privileges
- ❖ Trojan horse
- ❖ Social engineering
- ❖ Impersonation
- ❖ Exploits
- ❖ Systems
- ❖ Transitive trust
- ❖ Data driven
- ❖ Infrastructure
- ❖ Denial of service

As an IT Auditor which cloud models you have worked with?

❖ **Public:** Services are rendered over a network that is open for public use, example Amazon Elastic Compute Cloud (EC2)
❖ **Private:** private cloud is dedicated to a single organization
❖ **Community:** multi-tenant infrastructure
❖ **Hybrid:** Mix of private and public clouds

As an IT Auditor explain Transaction Authorization

Ensures all material transactions processed by the information system are valid and in accordance with management's objectives

As an IT Auditor, in terms of security how employee firings should be handled?

If employee has been actively trying to damage the company, company officials may be required to escort him off the premises for security reasons.

As an IT Auditor why should you consider renaming the Administrator account?

It is often the target of attacks because of its well-known name.

I will rename the Administrator account to an obscure name and create a "decoy" account called "Administrator" with no permissions.

Intruders will attempt to break in to this decoy account instead of the real account.
If the system is running Windows NT, though, you can use a hacker tool called Red Button to find out whether the Administrator account has been renamed, and if so, its new name

As an IT Auditor how will you turn off unused services on UNIX systems?

Edit /etc/inetd.conf file and Turn off unused services
What you have done to make UNIX/Linux Systems Secure?

- ❖ Turn off unused services
- ❖ Install IP filter or firewall rules

- ❖ Install ssh and tcpd
- ❖ Keep system up-to-date with the latest patches from your vendor
- ❖ UNIX File Sharing
- ❖ Screensaver for Unix/Linux desktop workstations

As an IT Auditor how will you prevent IP spoofing?

Egress filtering at the router most effectively prevents IP address spoofing; Egress filtering prevents you from sending unwanted traffic out to the Internet.

Here are ways to prevent IP address spoofing:

- ❖ Block IP Addresses
- ❖ Implement ACLS
- ❖ An Ingress Filter on All Internet Traffic,
- ❖ Egress ACLS

As an IT Auditor give some network security attacks examples that you have resolved?

- ❖ Email Based Network Security Attacks
- ❖ Logon Abuse Attacks
- ❖ Spoofing Attacks
- ❖ Intrusion Attacks
- ❖ Denial of Service (DoS) Network Security Attacks
- ❖ Worms & Trojans

As an IT Auditor explain the network security methods that you have used?

- ❖ Static Packet filter
- ❖ Stateful firewall
- ❖ Proxy Firewall
- ❖ IDS
- ❖ VPN device
- ❖ Intrusion detection system

As an IT Auditor explain the Principle of Default Deny?

- ❖ Firewall blocks all but explicitly allowed connections

- ❖ Shell access for users needs to be explicitly permitted

- ❖ All but necessary services are disabled

- ❖ All but necessary packages are removed

- ❖ Default configuration denies DHCP request from unknown clients

As an IT Auditor explain the Areas impacted by SOX

- ❖ Financial Reporting
- ❖ Corporate Governance
- ❖ Regulations on Role of Accounting

As an IT Auditor explain the penalties for Sox non-compliance?

- ❖ Loss of exchange listing
- ❖ Loss of Liability Insurance
- ❖ Fines
- ❖ Imprisonment
- ❖ Lack of investor confidence

What actions you as an IT Auditor can take to protect computer systems for client-side security while browsing the web?

- ❖ I will consult system support personnel if working from home
- ❖ I will always Use virus protection software
- ❖ I will always Use a firewall
- ❖ I will not open unknown email attachments
- ❖ I will not run programs of unknown origin
- ❖ I will disable hidden filename extensions
- ❖ I will keep all applications patched
- ❖ I will keep all operating system patched
- ❖ I will disconnect it from the network when not in use
- ❖ I will disable Java, JavaScript, and ActiveX if possible
- ❖ I will disable scripting features in email programs
- ❖ I will make regular backups of critical data
- ❖ I will make a boot disk in case computer is damaged

As an IT Auditor how will you secure the anonymous account?

- ❖ I will deny write access to Web content directories.
- ❖ I will make sure that it is not possible for this account to write to content directories
- ❖ I will restrict access to System tools.

❖ I will restrict access to command-line tools located in \WINNT\System32.
❖ I will assign permissions to groups instead of individual accounts.
❖ For the anonymous account, I will create a group and add the anonymous account to it and then explicitly deny access to the group for key directories and files

As an IT Auditor explain why application layer of TCP/IP stacks very weak link in terms of security?

Because that the application layer supports many protocols which provide many vulnerabilities and access points for attackers

How secure public Web servers running on Windows NT/2000?

I will disable NetBIOS and SMB.

NetBIOS is a broadcast-based, non-routable and insecure protocol.
Server Message Block (SMB) is an application-layer network protocol.
SMB provides shared access to files, printers, serial ports, and miscellaneous communications between hosts on a network
It is deployed in most Windows Platforms. An attacker can enumerate user accounts for the target system by inquiring the host/domain SID.

As an IT Auditor which services you should disable on a System running Windows OS?

❖ Alerter

❖ Application Layer Gateway Service

❖ Application Management

❖ Automatic Updates

- ❖ Background Intelligent Transfer Service

- ❖ Clip Book

- ❖ COM+ Event System

- ❖ COM+ System Application

- ❖ Computer Browser

- ❖ Cryptographic Services

- ❖ DHCP Client

- ❖ Distributed Link Tracking Client

Explain how will you make a UNIX or a Linux Server Secure?

- ❖ Preparation and Installation: If machine is a new install, I will protect it from hostile network traffic, until the operating system is installed and hardened.

- ❖ Patches and Additional Software
- ❖ I will apply the latest os patches.

- ❖ I will enable automatic notification of new patches.
- ❖ I will Minimize System Services.

- ❖ Kernel Tuning
- ❖ I will enable Stack Protection.
- ❖ I will Use better TCP Sequence numbers

- ❖ Logging
- ❖ I wll Turn on inetd tracing.
- ❖ I will capture messages sent to syslog AUTH facility.
- ❖ I will create /var/adm/loginlog.
- ❖ I will Log all failed login attempts.
- ❖ I will turn on croon logging.
- ❖ I will enable system accounting.
- ❖ System Access, Authentication, and Authorization
- ❖ I will secure Files/Directory Permissions/Access
- ❖ I will Verify passed, shadow, and group file permissions.
- ❖ I will disable login: prompts on serial ports.
- ❖ I will configure SSH.
- ❖ I will create /etc/ftpd/ftpusers
- ❖ I will Configure TCP Wrappers.
- ❖ I will restrict root logins to system console.
- ❖ I will verify that there are no accounts with empty password fields.
- ❖ I will set strong password enforcement policies.
- ❖ I will Verify no UID 0 accounts exist other than 'root'

- ❖ I will Install, configure, and use 'sudo' instead of 'su root'.

- ❖ Warning Banners
- ❖ I will create warning banners for standard login services.

- ❖ I will install software to check the integrity of critical operating system files.
- ❖ I will Install and enable anti-virus software.
- ❖ I will configure to update signature daily on AV.
- ❖ I will set up time synchronization using NTP.
- ❖ I will enable Process accounting at boot time.

As an IT security admin what action you will take to fix Shellshock vulnerability?

"Bash Bug" or "ShellShock," the GNU Bash Remote Code Execution Vulnerability (CVE-2014-6271) allows for remote code execution on servers via Bash, Bourne-Again Shell, security hole.

❖ I will update Bash to Patch Shellshock Bug by using command:

        Sudo yum update -y bash

❖ I will use detection systems based on real time intelligence gathered.

How to make a Windows server secure?

I will install only one Operating System on the server.
I will avoid dual boot configurations
I will make sure All partitions use NTFS, NTFS supports security properties and auditing
I will install system on its own volume and the data must reside on another partition than the system.
I will disable Services that should not be used by default:

  Help and Support
  IPSEC Services
  Print Spooler
  Windows Firewall/Internet Connection Sharing (ICS)
  Wireless Configuration

I will secure registry keys for the SNMP service. Only allow these accounts to access the keys: Administrators – Full Control
System – Full Control

❖ I will enforce password security:

❖ Enforce password history = 24 remembered
❖ Maximum password age = 42 days
❖ Minimum password age = 2 days
❖ Minimum password length = 8 characters
❖ Password must meet complexity requirements = Enabled
❖ Store password using reversible encryption = Disabled

❖ I will be hardening the Network Stack (tcp) as:

❖ EnableICMPRedirect = 0
❖ SynAttackProtect = 1
❖ EnableDeadGWDetect = 0
❖ EnablePMTUDiscovery = 0
❖ KeepAliveTime = 300,000
❖ DisableIPSourceRouting = 2
❖ TcpMaxConnectResponseRetransmissions = 2
❖ TcpMaxDataRetransmissions = 3
❖ PerformRouterDiscovery = 0
❖ TCPMaxPortsExhausted = 5

- ❖ I will tune Local Security Policy as:
- ❖ Audit Account Logon events Success, Failure
- ❖ Audit Account Management Success, Failure
- ❖ Audit Logon Events Success, Failure
- ❖ Audit Object Access Failure
- ❖ Audit Policy Change Success, Failure
- ❖ Audit Privilege Use Failure
- ❖ Audit System Events Success, Failure

I will enforce Event Log monitoring as:

I.   Maximum security log size – increase to allow for more in depth auditing
II.   Retention method for security log – set to "As needed" to ensure wrapping is FIFO in the removal cycle
  I. Shut down system immediately if unable to log – Set to "Disabled" to prevent shutdown

Explain what you will do for Securing Web Servers?

I.   I will isolate a Web server on a DMZ
II.   I will configure a Web server for access privileges
III.   I will Identify and enable Web server-specific logging tools
IV.   I will consider security appliances and tools
V.   I will configure authentication and encryption

What network performance metric you will analyze in case of Hack?

I will use performance monitoring to look for:
- ❖ Session,
- ❖ RTT (round-trip time)
- ❖ Server response time
- ❖ Retransmissions

As an IT security admin how will you secure a global company?

- ❖ I will use web filtering and network malware scanning
- ❖ I will implement a hybrid cloud solution:
- ❖ I will use Proxy appliances at each location for web filtering
- ❖ I will use Antivirus appliances scanning virus and malware

Explain how you will secure router and firewall systems?

- ❖ I will configure a loop back address
- ❖ I will monitor and handle SNMP with care
- ❖ I will avoid common names for password and naming schemes
- ❖ I will deploy logging about interface status, events, and debugging
- ❖ I will keep copy of current configurations of network devices in safe location
- ❖ I will never allow IP-directed broadcasts through the system
- ❖ I will configure devices with meaningful names
- ❖ I will Use a description for each interface
- ❖ I will specify bandwidth on the interfaces
- ❖ I will restrict data traffic to required ports and protocols only

What you recommend for securing databases?

- ❖ I will implement the Principle of Least Privilege
- ❖ I will stay up-to-date on patches
- ❖ I will Remove/disable unneeded default accounts
- ❖ I will implement Firewall/Access Control
- ❖ I will be Running Database processes under dedicated non-privileged account.
- ❖ I will add Password Security
- ❖ I will disable unneeded components
- ❖ I will tune Stored Procedures and Triggers; if X service doesn't need access to all tables in Y database then I will not give it access to all tables.
- ❖ I will not give accounts privileges that aren't needed
- ❖ I will be Throttling connections – making it harder for the bad guys to brute-force or guess passwords
    - ▪ I will Use firewall software like IPTables
    - ▪ I will Xinetd for throttling
- ❖ I will reduce the surface area of attack with firewall rules
- ❖ I will use Strong passwords

- ❖ I will be disabling unneeded components for databases
  - ▪ XML FTP (Oracle)
  - ▪ Named Pipes access (SQL Server)

Explain your experience with security audit?

I have performed a Gap analysis of the current security architecture. Examined site methodologies and practices.
I have performed Security Audits of:
- ❖ Host
- ❖ Firewall
- ❖ Networks
- ❖ Large networks

Name a few Audit Tools?

- ❖ SAINT/SATAN/ISS
- ❖ Nessus
- ❖ lsof /pff
- ❖ Nmap, tcpdump, ipsend
- ❖ MD5/DES/PGP

- ❖ COPS/Tiger
- ❖ Crack

How to Gather audit information?

- ❖ I will interview people
- ❖ I will review documentation
- ❖ I will perform technical investigation

What factors do you consider when you develop a budget?

- ❖ I will consider Projection from current expenses
- ❖ I will calculate Total Cost of Ownership (TCO)
- ❖ I will review IT Life Cycle
- ❖ I will use Benchmarking against peer organizations
- ❖ I will do Mission-driven, top-down planning

Explain what components you will use in network security system?

- ❖ Firewall
- ❖ I will use Packet-filter firewall to filter at the network or transport layer
- ❖ I will use Proxy firewall to filter at the application layer
- ❖ NAT
- ❖ I will use NAT to solve the problem of IP address limitation
- ❖ I will use NAT to Provide load balance and redundancy
- ❖ IDS
- ❖ I will use IDS for Active detection to monitor the network status
- ❖ I will use three methods: signature, statistical and integrity
- ❖ I will use four types of IDS: host, network, applications and integrity
- ❖ Honey pots
- ❖ I will use it To Attract Hackers

Why you need Digital signatures?

It ensures the integrity, authenticity, and support for non-repudiation related to data.

List Cryptosystems Types?

I.   Asymmetric Cryptosystems
II.   Symmetric Cryptosystems

Explain the Advantages and disadvantages of public-key cryptography?

The main advantage of public-key cryptography is increased security, convenience, key distribution. Another major advantage of public-key systems is that they can provide a method for digital signatures.

A disadvantage of using public-key cryptography for encryption is speed,
Private keys never need to be transmitted or revealed to anyone.

In asymmetric or public key, cryptography there is no need for exchanging keys, thus eliminating the key distribution problem.

DES encryption length? Why it's not used now? Whats the alternative?

DES encryption algorithm uses a 56 bit key to encrypt data for transit.
Automated attacks at guessing all possible keys have been reported so
DES is not used anymore as it is an old, weak and broken encryption algorithm, and was replaced by 3DES. AES is the standard and is being used as of today and proves to be safe and a strong symmetric encryption algorithm.

In Windows how IPSec is implemented?

IPSec is implemented primarily as an administrative tool that you can use to enforce security policies on IP network traffic.

What is a security policy? Mechanism?

Set of IT security rules that will protect IT environment. A packet filtering is a mechanism for implementing network security policies. It is recognized at the IP layer.

What action defines security requirements?

A filter action defines the security requirements for the network traffic.

What modes filters can be set?

A filter action can be configured to:
Permit, Block, or Negotiate security (negotiate IPSec).

Where IPSec filters work?

IPSec filters are inserted into the IP layer of the computer TCP/IP networking protocol stack so that they can examine (filter) all inbound or outbound IP packets.

IPsec Services?

IPsec offers two services, authentication and encryption.

DMZ Contains what components?

Web server
Mail server

Application gateway
E-commerce systems

Is DMZ Secure?

Yes, because DMZ supports network and application level security in addition to providing a secure place to host your public servers.

What are authentication protocols? Name them?

A cryptographic protocol with the purpose of authenticating entities wishing to communicate securely.

- ❖ AKA
- ❖ CAVE-based_authentication
- ❖ Challenge-handshake authentication protocol (CHAP)
- ❖ CRAM-MD5
- ❖ Diameter
- ❖ NTP
- ❖ PAP

- ❖ CHAP
- ❖ Extensible Authentication Protocol (EAP)
- ❖ Host Identity Protocol (HIP)
- ❖ Kerberos
- ❖ MS-CHAP and MS-CHAPv2 variants of CHAP
- ❖ LAN Manager
- ❖ NTLM, also known as NT LAN Manager
- ❖ Password-authenticated key agreement protocols
- ❖ Password Authentication Protocol (PAP)
- ❖ Protected Extensible Authentication Protocol (PEAP)
- ❖ RADIUS
- ❖ Secure Remote Password protocol (SRP)
- ❖ TACACS and TACACS+
- ❖ RFID-Authentication Protocols
- ❖ Woo Lam 92 (protocol)

What is Socks? Benefits of Socks version 5 proxy server?

Socks are a circuit-layer proxy protocol used in client/server networking environments.
Socks v5 supports authentication to the proxy server, IP version 6 addressing, and domain names.

What is an IP directed broadcast? Use?

IP directed broadcast is an IP packet whose destination address is a valid broadcast address for some IP subnet, but it originates from a node that is not itself part of that destination subnet. If IP Directed Broadcast is not available the packets destined for the broadcast IP address of any interface connected to a router will be dropped.

Access Lists should be used in conjunction with directed broadcast. For example Windows PCs Network Neighborhood resources will be missing in the absence of this.

Why tftp is insecure?

Because tftp does not require a logon id and password to connect to the server and ftp does.

802.11b supports what encrypted standard?

802.11b supports an encrypted standard known as Wired Equivalent Privacy (WEP)

Why you should Restrict Access to the IIS Anonymous Account?

Attackers target this well known account to perform malicious actions.

Name a network sniffer

I.   tcpdump
II.   nit sniff

What is ICMP bombing?

ICMP Internet Control Message Protocol is used by routers to notify a host when a
Destination is unreachable Attacker can bomb a host by forging ICMP-unreachable.

What you suggest for PC for client-side security that is used for browsing the web?

  I will recommend using virus protection software
  I will recommend using a firewall
  I will recommend not opening unknown email attachments
  I will recommend not running programs of unknown origin
  I will Disable hidden filename extensions
  I will keep all applications patched

I will keep operating system patched to the current levels

I will Turn off your computer or disconnect from the network when not in use
I will disable Java, JavaScript, and ActiveX if possible
I will disable scripting features in email programs
I will make regular backups of critical data
I will make a boot disk in case computer is damaged or compromised

Which test file can be used to determine if an anti-virus scanner is working?

EICAR allows users to check whether their antivirus software is running.

How to find if your computer has a macro virus? How to resolve it?

In my experience being unable to save a document in Microsoft Word means computer may have a macro virus. Microsoft Word documents can use macros, which can potentially carry these viruses. To minimize this possibility, I will activate the built-in macro protection tool.

Security token combines which two factors?

Security tokens provide an extra level of assurance through a method known as two-factor authentication: the user has a personal identification number (PIN).

How the LANMAN challenge/response and NTLMv1 protocols authenticate users?

NTLM (NT LAN Manager) is a suite of Microsoft security protocols that provides authentication, integrity, and confidentiality to users.

- ❖ **First a client sends an authentication request to the server.**
- ❖ **Then a protocol negotiation occurs between the client and server.**
- ❖ **Then the server sends the client 8-byte challenge a pseudo-random number.**
- ❖ **Then the client sends a 24-byte response.**

❖ Then the server authenticates the client.

How a Screening Router provides security?

It Filters traffic passing between one network and another, Performs IP forwarding, based on an access control list (ACL)

What are Infrastructure attacks?

Potential attacks on core Internet infrastructure .TCP sequence guessing or "the Mitnick Attack". If an attacker knows the sequence numbers of a connection stream he can
Generate correct-looking packets by examining the TCP sequence number received for one connection; Primary target: the rsh command, which relied on address-based Authentication.

How to secure Wireless Router?

Disable wireless administrating, change the setting that allows administrating the router through a wireless connection to 'off' .One will require connecting with a LAN cable for administration. This disables any wireless hacking into the router. The most secure means of administering a router is a Serial Connection.

What Ports are for Echo and Chargen services?

Echo service (port 7) and chargen (port 19)

What is Chargen?

Chargen is short for Character Generator and is a service that generates random characters either in one UDP packet containing a random number (between 0 and 512) of characters, or a TCP session. The UDP Chargen server looks for a UDP packet on port 19 and responds with the random character packet.

What is a " Belt and Suspenders" approach in IT Security?

It's about layering your IT security defenses to guard against single points of failure; in my opinion the "Belt and Suspenders" approach to security installs redundant layers of security to the system. It's based on the idea that if your belt gives way, the suspenders are still there to hold your pants up. For example in belt-and-suspenders firewall, the gateway machine sits on two different Networks, between the two filtering routers.

What are two uses of the TCP wrappers package?

The TCP Wrappers package provides host-based access control to network services & provides granular access control to TCP services.

When a connection attempt is made to a TCP-wrapped service, the service first references the host's access files (/etc/hosts. allow and /etc/hosts. deny) to determine whether or not the client is allowed to connect. It logs all TCP connections. In most cases, it then uses the syslog daemon (syslogd) to write the name of the requesting client and the requested service to /var/log/secure or /var/log/messages.

What is NAT?

Network address translation (NAT) takes IP addresses used on one network and translates them into IP addresses used within another network.

One use of NAT is to hide network addresses from hosts on another network.

As an IT Auditor Accounting Records

Consist of documents, journals, and ledgers

As an IT Auditor why you suggest Access Control

Ensures only authorized personnel have access to the firm's assets

As an IT Auditor why you suggest Independent Verification

Independent checks of the accounting system to identify errors and misrepresentations

As an IT Auditor why you suggest Application Controls

I. **Ensure validity, completeness, and accuracy of financial transactions**
II. **Application specific**

As an IT Auditor why you suggest General Controls

I. Not application specific
II. Apply to all systems

As an IT Auditor list Data Processing Elements

❖ Data control - receives hard copy source documents from end users and transcribes them into digital computer processing in batch systems
❖ Computer operations - electronic files produced in data conversion are later processed by the central computer
❖ Data library - room adjacent to computer center that provides safe storage fro the off-line data files

As an IT Auditor list Incompatible IT Functions

- ❖ Systems development from computer operations
- ❖ Database administration from other functions
- ❖ New systems development from maintenance

As an IT Auditor list DDP Risks

- ❖ Insufficient use of resources
- ❖ Performed by end users
- ❖ Destruction of audit trails
- ❖ Inadequate segregation of duties of incompatible functions
- ❖ Hiring qualified professionals
- ❖ Credentials of applicants
- ❖ Lack of standards

As an IT Auditor list DDP Advantages

- ❖ Cost reductions
- ❖ Improved cost control responsibility
- ❖ Improved user satisfaction
- ❖ Backup flexibility
- ❖ Corporate IT Function

As an IT Auditor list DDP Controls

- ❖ Central testing of commercial software and hardware
- ❖ User services
- ❖ Standard-setting body
- ❖ Personnel review

As an IT Auditor list types of Cloud Computing

Location-independent computing whereby shared data centers deliver hosted IT services over the internet

- ❖ Software-as-a-Service (SaaS)
- ❖ Infrastructure-as-a-service (IaaS)
- ❖ Platform-as-a-service (PaaS)

As an IT Auditor Cloud Computing Implementation Issues

Cloud computing is designed as one-size-fits-all solution

As an IT Auditor list the threats to Operating System Integrity

- ❖ Privileged personnel who abuse authority
- ❖ Individuals, both internal and external, who browse the operating system to identify and exploit security flaws
- ❖ Individuals who intentionally or accidentally insert computer viruses or other forms of destructive programs into the operating system

As an IT Auditor which illegal denial-of-service (DoS) attacks you are familiar with?

- ❖ Denial of Service: Smurf Attack
- ❖ Denial of Service: Syn-Flood Attack
- ❖ Denial of Service: DDoS

As an IT Auditor list some Computer-Aided Audit Tools

- ❖ Test data method
- ❖ Base case approach
- ❖ Tracing
- ❖ Integrated Test Facility
- ❖ Parallel simulation

Give some Examples of unnecessary services?

- ❖ FTP
- ❖ Telephony
- ❖ Telnet
- ❖ Rlogin

As an IT Auditor name three steps in the audit process?

- ❖ Understanding the Audit Objective
- ❖ The Audit Scope
- ❖ Audit Risk Assessment

Name three types of audit

- ❖ Information System Audit (IT Audit),
- ❖ Integrated Audit and

❖ Financial Audit

As an IT Auditor how will you test the operating effectiveness of the controls?

❖ Inquiry
❖ Observation
❖ Examination of Evidence
❖ Performance

As an IT Auditor what are the sources of IT Risk?

❖ Human Factors
❖ IT Processes
❖ IT Technical Configuration

As an IT Auditor Define information assurance

The Information and related Assets are:

I. Processed Securely (Meaning they have information integrity, reliability, and validity)

II. The Technology Assets are managed efficiently and effectively

As an IT Auditor Identify Key Components of COSO Framework

❖ Control Environment
❖ Risk Assessment
❖ Control Activities

- ❖ Information & Communication
- ❖ Monitoring Activities

As an IT Auditor what values you can add to Organization

I. Cop
II. Investigator
III. Partner and Trusted Advisor

As an IT Auditor Identify factors of internal controls

I. Policies
II. Procedures
III. Information system

As an IT Auditor Identify types of IT controls?

I. Preventative
II. Detective

III. Corrective

As an IT Auditor Identify factors defining a material misstatement

I. Likelihood
II. Magnitude
III. Pervasiveness

As an IT Auditor Identify factors of IT controls?

I. Preventative
II. Detective
III. Corrective

As an IT Auditor can you recognize the layers of *OSI MODEL*

7 layer model that describes how data moves from one system to another system.

- ❖ **Layer 1 :Physical Link- example : cables, Network Interface Cards**

- ❖ **Layer 2 :Data Link- example : Switches, Mac addressing Protocols- PPTP, Token Ring**

- ❖ **Layer 3: Network- Logical or IP addressing example : Determines best path for the destination**
  Protocols- IPv4, IPv6, ICMP, IPsec

- ❖ **Layer 4: Transport- example : Defines ports and Reliability Protocols- TCP, UDP**

- ❖ **Layer 5: Session- Starts and ends session and also keeps them isolated**
  Protocol- example : SMB, NFS, Socks

- ❖ **Layer 6 :Presentation- example : Type of Data; HTTPS; encryption services**

- ❖ **Layer 7: Application- example: Web browser (Internet explorer, Mozilla, google chrome.)**

Protocols- DNS, DHCP, HTTP, FTP, IMAP, LDAP, NTP, Radius, SSH, SMTP, SNMP, Telnet, TFTP

As an IT Auditor can you identify the objectives of disaster recovery planning?

- ❖ Minimize the destruction or loss of data
- ❖ Establish another way to process information
- ❖ Resume normal operations as soon as possible
- ❖ Train and familiarize employees with the plan

As an IT Auditor can you identify Cloud Computing Services

I. SaaS (Microsoft office)

II. IaaS (computing resource use)
III. PaaS (canvas)

As an IT Auditor can you identify threats of Cyber security

I. Interruptions
II. Interceptions
III. Modification
IV. Fabrication

As an IT Auditor can you identify 2 Security Concepts around Data

I. Confidentiality,
II. System Availability

As an IT Auditor what improvements you recommend in password controls?

- ❖ Complexity
- ❖ Expiration
- ❖ Lockout
- ❖ Monitoring
- ❖ Audit Logging
- ❖ Account Sharing
- ❖ History

As an IT Auditor can you identify the IT duties that should be segregated?

- ❖ Systems analyst
- ❖ Programmer

- ❖ Operator
- ❖ Librarian
- ❖ Security

As an IT Auditor can you Identify and assess controls for hardware and systems software.

- ❖ Parity check
- ❖ Echo check
- ❖ Diagnostic routines
- ❖ Boundary protection

As an IT Auditor can you identify and assess categories of general controls.

- ❖ Organization and operation
- ❖ Systems development and documentation
- ❖ Hardware and systems software
- ❖ Access
- ❖ Data and procedures

As an IT Auditor can you identify control totals?

I. Batch totals
II. Hash totals
III. Record count

As an IT Auditor can you identify logic checks?

I. Limit tests
II. Validity checks
III. Missing data checks
IV. Check digits

As an IT Auditor can you identify Physical Controls

❖ Independent Verification
❖ Transaction Authorization
❖ Segregation of Duties
❖ Supervision
❖ Accounting Records
❖ Access Control

As an IT Auditor can you identify IT Controls

I. General Controls
II. Application Controls

As an IT Auditor can you identify the Five Assertions

❖ Existence or Occurrence
❖ Completeness
❖ Rights and Obligations
❖ Valuation or Allocation
❖ Presentation of Disclosure

AS AN IT AUDITOR can you identify the TYPES OF AUDIT RISK

(Inherent, Control, and Detection)

I. Associated with unique characteristics of clients business/industry

    II. Likelihood that the control structure is flawed because controls aren't there or are inadequate to prevent/detect errors

   III. Risk auditors are willing to take that errors not detected or prevented by the control structure will not be detected by the auditor

As an IT Auditor can you identify web application risks?

     I. Input validation
    II. Session management
   III. Authentication
   IV. Authorization
    V. Data protection

As an IT Auditor can you identify components of a computer-based IT Audit?

I. Procedures
II. People
III. Databases
IV. Hardware
V. Software
VI. Data Communications

As an IT Auditor can you identify 5 techniques to audit computerized AIS- *ACCOUNTING INFORMATION SYSTEM*?

I. Testing Computer Programs
II. Validating Computer Programs
III. Review Of Systems Software
IV. Validating Users/Access Privileges
V. Continuous Auditing

As an IT Auditor can you identify significant risks around data security related risks?

    I. Confidentiality
   II. System Availability

As an IT Auditor can you identify significant risks about generic accounts?

You lose accountability over who performs actions

As an IT Auditor which threats you will look for in cyber security audit

    I. Interruptions
   II. Interceptions

III. Modification
IV. Fabrication

As an IT Auditor which Data Security Concepts you will validate?

  I. Consistency
 II. Integrity
III. Accuracy

As an IT Auditor which parts of the fraud triangle you are familiar with?

  I. Opportunities

II. Pressure/Incentive
III. Rationalization

As an IT Auditor Identify concepts of IDM

Identity and Access Management

    I. Identity
   II. Entitlements
 III. Provisioning
 IV. Enforcement

As an IT Auditor what you suggest for Provisioning

   I. Process of an Identity's Creation
  II. Change
 III. Termination

IV. Approval

As an IT Auditor what Enforcement and verification of IT controls you suggest?

Enforcement of (IDM)

Enforcement and verification of IT controls
  I. **Authentication**
  II. **Authorization**
  III. **Logging of identities**

As an IT Auditor Identify standard steps in the IDM process?

  I. **Request Submission**
  II. **Request Approval**
  III. **Provisioning of Access**
  IV. **Entitlement Repository**

As an IT Auditor Identify PCI Requirements?

    I.   Firewall
   II.   Protect Stored Data
  III.   Encrypt Data
  IV.   Use Anti-Virus Software
   V.   Restrict Physical Access

As an IT Auditor what data protection techniques you recommend?

    I.   I will implement Physical Security
   II.   I will ensure successful Back-Ups
  III.   I will implement Security Software
  IV.   I will ensure Personal Responsibility

As an IT Auditor Identify steps you will perform in an investigation for data?

I. I will find what occurred
II. I will prove the loss
III. I will figure out responsibility
IV. I will figure out intent

As an IT Auditor Identify factors impacting IDM

Identity and Access Management

I. Identity
II. Entitlements
III. Provisioning
IV. Enforcement

As an IT Auditor Identify factors impacting Provisioning

I. Process of an Identity's Creation
II. Change
III. Termination
IV. Approval

As an IT Auditor Identify factors impacting Enforcement

I. Authentication
II. Authorization
III. Logging of identities as they are used in an IT system

As an IT Auditor identify the steps in the IDM process?

I. Request Submission

II. Request Approval
III. Provisioning of Access

As an IT Auditor identify the Methods for conducting a security control assessment

I. I will conduct Examination
II. I will conduct Interview
III. I will conduct Test

As an IT Auditor identify the closely-related areas of Compliance?

I. Risk management
II. Governance
III. Legal Governance
IV. Risk Management
V. Compliance

As an IT Auditor identify the impacts of audits and assessments?

I. Audits can result in blaming an individual
II. *BLAME* allocation: should protect against the risk of being blamed for failure

As an IT Auditor identify the impacts of Noncompliance with regulatory standards?

I. Brand damage: reputation risk
II. Fines: penalties and interest
III. Imprisonment: sentencing

As an IT Auditor Identify factors impacting hardware and systems software

I. Parity check
II. Echo check
III. Diagnostic routines
IV. Boundary protection

As an IT Auditor Identify categories of general controls

I. Organization and operation
II. Systems development and documentation
III. Hardware and systems software
IV. Access
V. Data and procedures

As an IT Auditor Identify factors impacting control totals

I. Batch totals
II. Hash totals
III. Record count

As an IT Auditor Identify factors impacting general controls

I. Organization and operation
II. Systems development and documentation
III. Hardware and systems software
IV. Access
V. Data and procedures

As an IT Auditor List some internal control implications associated with an IT environment.

    I. Segregation of duties may be undermined
   II. Audit trail may be lacking
  III. Computer processing is uniform

As an IT Auditor List the types of physical safeguards used to protect the data files?

    I. File labels: color-coded *LABEL* and *FILING* systems
   II. File protection rings: *FILE PROTECTION RINGS* or boundary *PROTECTION*
  III. File protection plans: solutions that proactively secure and control access

As an IT Auditor which IT duties you will keep segregated

    I.   Systems analyst
   II. Programmer
  III. Operator
  IV. Librarian
   V. Security

What is ICMP? What is ICMP bombing?

ICMP is Internet Control Message Protocol, used by routers to notify a host when a
Destination is unreachable using "ping". ICMP Bombing includes forged messages such as EOF, dead socket, redirect, etc. also known as Nuking. The goal of the of this attack is to saturate the victims network with ICMP traffic and waste all his CPU time on replying to our spoofed packets.

As an IT Auditor List some examples of logic checks

I. Limit tests: A computer program step that compares data with predetermined limits as a reasonableness test
II. Validity checks: control over input of data to a computer system
III. Missing data checks: probability distribution of missingness, value is missing
IV. Check digits: redundancy check for error detection

As an IT Auditor which Steps in BCP create an effective business continuity plan

I. Business Impact Analysis (BIA)
II. Risk assessment
III. Risk mitigation

IV. Risk Monitoring

As an IT Auditor what factors you Consider of a BCP?

I. Completeness: Review the accuracy and completeness
II. Relevance: The Future Relevance of Audit
III. Approval: Audit Committee is required to approve

As an IT Auditor what factors will you consider for Disaster Planning?

I. Disaster Recovery Site: A disaster recovery site (DR site) is an alternative backup facility
II. Data Recovery Plan: Disaster recovery plan a set of documents detailing the steps and procedures to be followed in the event of a disaster.
III. Production Site: a hot site is a complete copy of your production site

As an IT Auditor how will you tackle fraud?

I. I will make sure that the assessment and identification of residual and inherent risk by control measures and mitigation of risk measures

II. I will enhance the effectiveness and relevance of assurance by detection and monitoring management tools.

III. I will strengthen the controls to avoid errors and frauds.

IV. I will form a fraud and investigation team in identification, assessment, investigation and monitoring of suspicious transactions

As an IT Auditor can you Identify application control objectives and how to achieve it?

Objectives:

I. To ensure input data is accurate, complete, authorized, and correct.

II. To ensure data is processed as intended in an acceptable time period.
III. To ensure data stored is accurate and complete.
IV. To ensure outputs are accurate and complete.
V. To ensure a record is maintained that tracks the process of data

To achieve the above objectives:

I. I will Conduct the audit
II. I will perform a risk assessment
III. I will determine the scope of the review
IV. I will develop and communicate the detailed review plan
V. I will determine the need for specialized resources
VI. I will use computer-assisted audit techniques

As an IT Auditor can you Identify IT Audit Methodologies

I. CobiT
II. BS 7799 - Code of Practice (CoP)
III. BSI - IT Baseline Protection Manual
IV. ITSEC
V. Common Criteria (CC)

As an IT Auditor can you Identify CobiT - Structure

I. Domains
II. PO - Planning & Organization
III. processes (high-level control objectives)
IV. AI - Acquisition & Implementation
V. processes (high-level control objectives)
VI. DS - Delivery & Support
VII. processes (high-level control objectives)
VIII. M - Monitoring
IX. processes (high-level control objectives)

CobiT control model covers:
I. Security (Confidentiality, Integrity, Availability)
II. Fiduciary (Effectiveness, Efficiency, Compliance, Reliability of Information)
III. IT Resources (Data, Application Systems, Technology, Facilities, People)

As an IT Auditor can you Identify CobiT - IT Process Matrix

CobiT - IT'S Process Matrix
- ❖ Information Criteria
- ❖ Effectiveness
- ❖ Efficiency
- ❖ Confidentiality
- ❖ Integrity
- ❖ Availability
- ❖ Compliance
- ❖ Reliability

As an IT Auditor can you Identify IT Resources

- ❖ People
- ❖ Applications
- ❖ Technology
- ❖ Facilities
- ❖ Data

As an IT Auditor can you Identify

Control Categories

- ❖ Information security policy
- ❖ Security organization
- ❖ Assets classification & control
- ❖ Personnel security
- ❖ Physical & environmental security
- ❖ Computer & network management
- ❖ System access control
- ❖ Systems development & maintenance
- ❖ Business continuity planning
- ❖ Compliance

As an IT Auditor can you Identify

Key Controls

- ❖ Information security policy document
- ❖ Allocation of information security responsibilities
- ❖ Information security education and training
- ❖ Reporting of security incidents
- ❖ Virus controls
- ❖ Business continuity planning process

- ❖ Control of proprietary software copying
- ❖ Safeguarding of organizational records
- ❖ Data protection
- ❖ Compliance with security policy

As an IT Auditor can you Identify BSI - Security Measures

- ❖ Protection for generic components
- ❖ Infrastructure
- ❖ Non-networked systems
- ❖ LANs
- ❖ Data transfer systems
- ❖ Telecommunications
- ❖ Other IT components

As an IT Auditor Identify audit trails records useful for maintaining security and for recovering lost data

Information gained by audit trails
- ❖ Usernames, ip addresses, motives, event timelines, what people did and what computers were accessed
- ❖ Network forensics
- ❖ Network administrators can use audit trail data to solve data mysteries
- ❖ Information gained by network forensics
- ❖ Identify data leaks, prevent security attacks, alert real time administrators
- ❖ Network policies
- ❖ Help the company to run smoothly with rules in place to deter security breaches
- ❖ Audit trail should contain enough
- ❖ Information to allow management, the auditor and the user:
- ❖ User identification
- ❖ Type of event

❖ **Date and time**
❖ **Success or failure indication**
❖ **Origination of event**
❖ **Identity or name of affected data, system component, or resource**

What is ITIL?

The Information Technology Infrastructure Library (ITIL) is a framework of best practices.
The concepts within ITIL support information technology services delivery organizations with the planning of consistent, documented, and repeatable or customized processes that improve service delivery to the business.

ITIL framework consists of which processes?

1. Service Support (Service Desk, Incident Management, Problem Management, Change Management, Configuration Management, and Release Management)

2. Services Delivery (Service Level Management, Capacity Management, Availability Management, Financial Management and ITS Service Continuity Management).

Explain one benefit of ITIL?

The quality and the costs of the IT services can be controlled more efficiently.

What are the benefits of implementing a service desk?

1. Increased first call resolution
2. Improved tracking of service quality
3. Improved recognition of trends and incidents
4. Improved employee satisfaction
5. Skill based support
6. Rapidly restore service
7. Improved incident response time
8. Quick service restoration

What Processes are utilized by the Service Desk?

Workflow and procedures diagrams

What is the objective of Incident Management?

Minimize the disruption to the business by restoring service operations to agreed levels as quickly as possible.

What are the Benefits of an Incident Management Process?

1. Incident detection and recording
2. Classification and initial support
3. Investigation and diagnosis
4. Resolution and recovery
5. Incident closure
6. Incident ownership, monitoring, tracking and communication
7. Repeatable Process

Capacity Management processes?

1. Performance monitoring
2. Workload monitoring
3. Application Sizing ITIL
4. Resource forecasting
5. Demand forecasting
6. Modeling

How will you test connectivity between workstations?

I will use ping command to check connectivity.
Syntax
    PING [options] destination host

Ping verifies connectivity by sending Internet Control Message Protocol (ICMP).

What are the main components of a computer?

    I. Motherboard
    II. CPU (central processing unit)
    III. RAM (random access memory)
    IV. Video card
    V. Optical drive
    VI. Power supply
    VII. Hard disk
    VIII. ROM (read only memory)

How will you verify there are duplicate IP addresses?

I will use arp command.

ARP - Address Resolution Protocol

Display and modify the IP-to-Physical address translation tables used by address resolution protocol.

```
Syntax
   View the contents of the local ARP cache table
      ARP -a [ip_addr] [-N if_addr]
```

How to view and manage hardware devices and their device drivers in Windows?

I have used device manager to view hardware resources, interrupt request (IRQ), I/O port address, memory address, and Direct Memory Access (DMA) settings.

I have used Device manager to View:
IRQs
Hidden devices
NIC

I have used Device manager to
Update driver
Disable
Uninstall
Scan for changes

List three devices that are contained inside the computer case.

What computer parts are inside the box?

I. Motherboard
II. Cooling System
III. RAM
IV. CPU
V. PSU
VI. Hard Drive

How will you verify configuration information about the system, such as date and time, CPU, hard drives or floppy drives?

CMOS setup   or BIOS

Have you recovered a system by Recovery Console?

Yes.

Recovery Console is a diagnostic tool that I have used to fix major Windows XP/2000 problems.

It's a command-line interface that provides administrative tools useful for recovering a system that is not booting correctly.

It allows me to view disk volumes, format drives, read and write data and perform other administrative tasks.

I have used these Recovery Console Commands:

Diskpart: Manages partitions on your hard drives.

Fixboot: Writes a new partition boot sector onto the specified partition.

Fixmbr: Repairs the master boot record of the specified disk.

Format: Formats a disk.

Systemroot: Sets the current directory to the systemroot directory

When have you used Safe Mode?

I have used for troubleshooting or diagnostic purposes because it's an advanced boot option allowing a Windows system to be booted with minimal services or drivers loaded,

Explain Subnet Mask?

I. It's the number used in a TCP/IP address scheme that masks off the host portion from the IP address, leaving only the network portion.

II. A Subnet mask is a 32-bit number that masks an IP address, and divides the IP address into network address and host address.

How do you know if there is an intermittent problem with the electrical system?

I. The computer stops
II. Hangs.
III. Reboots
IV. Motherboard fails
V. The power supply overheats

How to verify how devices are managed?

By using:

I. DMA
II. IQ
III. IRQ
IV. Memory

Explain Driver Signing?

It's applying a digital signature to a driver as a means of quality control or verification.

How will you examine and configure all the hardware and drivers installed on a machine?

I will use the Device Manager to manage all the hardware on a computer that Windows is aware of.

To launch Device Manager:

I will use the following command: devmgmt.msc

Explain your experience with RAID?

RAID=Redundancy Array of Inexpensive/Independent Disks, provides reliable overall storage subsystem than can be achieved by a single disk.

I have used these types of RAID levels:

Raid Level 0 Striping with no mirroring or parity
Raid Level 1 Mirroring with no striping, it provides improved fault tolerance
Raid Level 5 Striping with parity over multiple disks, performance, and fault tolerance.

What is BIA? What Business Continuity Components you will focus on?

A business impact analysis (BIA) can provide true costs of downtime and business disruptions for a particular business.

Business Continuity Components
    I. People
   II. Property
  III. Systems
  IV. Data

Why UNIX is widely used?

It has these features:

        I. Multitasking.
       II. Multi-user.
      III. Portability.
     IV. Network applications.

Are you familiar with UNIX commands?

Yes.

I have used many UNIX commands such as:

ls	lists directory information
pwd	lists current directory
cd	change directory
grep	Builds substrings with out data stream/files
wc	counts the number of words, line, and bytes in a file
cp	copy
mv	move
chown	change owner
chgrp	change group
chmod	change the permissions of the file

cat   print the whole file
xargs   execute arguments
find   find files
grep   find things inside files
man   read a manual page

What is a computer virus?

It's a computer program that infects a computer without the permission or knowledge of the user.

What preventative maintenances have you performed?

   I. Updates
   II. Backup

What are the Information Classification levels?

The Information Classification levels are (from highest to lowest):
   I.   Trade Secret.
   II. Sensitive.
   III. Private.
   IV. Confidential.
   V.   Public

What Security modes have you worked on?

The four modes of operation: dedicated mode, system-high mode, compartmented mode,
and multilevel mode.

What is Certificate Authority?

A certificate authority (CA) is an authority in a network that issues and manages security credentials and public keys for message encryption.

What does a certificate contains?

The certificate usually contains the server name, the trusted certificate.

How to calculate Security Risk?

Risk = Threat x Vulnerability x Cost

What are the common issues with vulnerability assessment tools?

    I. Expensive
   II. Infrequent
  III. Time consuming to set up and operate
  IV. High false positive rates
   V. Cause network resource issues

What are the classes of attacks against SANs?

Snooping, Spoofing, Denial of Service.

What are the Classification criteria for data security?

Value; age; useful life; personal association.

What is IANA?

The Internet Assigned Numbers Authority (IANA) is responsible for maintaining the official assignments of port numbers for specific uses.

Explain your experience with NFS?

NFS is inherently insecure. While certain methods of encrypted authentication exist, all data is transmitted in the clear, and accounts may be spoofed by user programs.

I only use NFS within a highly trusted environment, behind the appropriate firewalls and with careful attention to host security. I Disable NFS if possible. NFS traffic flows in cleartext (even when using "AUTH_DES" or "AUTH_KERB" for authentication) so any files transported via NFS are susceptible to snooping.

What is the role of Application layer?

The Application layer provides network services directly to the user's application such as a web browser, email software and Windows Explorer.

This layer is said to be "closest to the user".

Protocols that operate on this layer include: TELNET, HTTP, FTP, TFTP, SMTP, NTP, SNMP, and EDI.

What is Cramming?

"Cramming" is the practice of placing unauthorized, misleading or deceptive charges on your telephone bill. Cramming is a form of fraud in which small charges are added to a bill.

Explain RC4 with MD5?

RC4 cipher with 128-bit encryption and MD5 message authentication. RC4 ciphers are the fastest ciphers.

This cipher, because it has 128-bit encryption, is the second strongest cipher next to Triple DES (Data Encryption Standard) with 168-bit encryption.

Examples of Denial of Service (DOS) Attacks?

1. Transmission Failure
    a. Line cut
    b. Network noise making a packet unrecognizable or undeliverable
2. Connection Flooding
    a. Sending too much data
    b. Protocol attacks: TCP, UDP, ICMP (Internet Control Message Protocol)
3. Echo-Chargen
    a. Attack works between two hosts
4. Ping of Death
    a. Flood network with ping packets

        b. Attack limited by the smallest bandwidth to
            victim
  5. Smurf
        a. It is a variation of ping attack
  6. Syn Flood
        a. Attack uses the TCP protocol suite

What is CVE?

The Common Vulnerabilities and Exposures or CVE system
provides a reference-method for publicly known information-
security vulnerabilities and exposures.

What is *SALAMI ATTACK*?

 A SALAMI ATTACK is a series of minor attacks that collectively
result in a larger attack.

What does Multipartite Virus mean?

A multipartite virus is a fast-moving virus that uses file
infectors or boot infectors to attack the boot sector and
executable files simultaneously

What is Separation of Duties?

Separation of duties (SoD) is the concept of having more than
one person required to complete a task.

Whats polymorphic virus?

A polymorphic virus is one that encrypts its code differently with each infection, or generation of infections.

What types of firewalls you know?

Conceptually, there are three types of firewalls: Network layer; Application layer; Hybrids

What is DAC - Discretionary Access Control?

Discretionary Access Control (DAC) is a means of restricting access to objects based upon the identity of users and/or groups to which they belong.

Well known ports?

0-1023

Explain Ping Of Death? How to send it?

A ping is normally 32 bytes in size.
Its 84 bytes when the Internet Protocol [IP] header is considered.
I have seen many computer systems could not handle a ping packet larger than the maximum IPv4 packet size, which is 65,535 bytes.

A ping of death (abbreviated "POD") is a type of attack on a computer that involves sending a malformed or otherwise malicious ping to a computer.

Sending a ping of this size could crash the target computer is called Ping of Death.
It is also called long ICMP.

Syntax

PING [options] destination_host

PING -L 65536 destination_host
Have you used Tripwire?

Tripwire is a free software security and data integrity tool useful for monitoring and alerting on specific file change(s) on a range of systems.

What is ROT13?

ROT13 ("rotate by 13 places", sometimes hyphenated ROT-13) is a simple substitution cipher.

Explain Source Quench?

Source quench is used to temporarily decrease the amount of data transferred.

EXPLAIN TROJAN HORSE?

Trojan horse is a program in which malicious or harmful code is contained inside apparently harmless programming.

A Trojan horse is a program that poses as a useful or legitimate program, but turns out to be malicious code.

  I.   Different types of Trojans are :
  II. Remote access Trojans (rats)
  III. Backdoor Trojans (backdoors)
  IV. IRC Trojans (ircbots)
  V.   Keylogging Trojans

Explain the major difference(s) between block and stream ciphers?

A block cipher would break up a clear text into fixed-length blocks and then proceed to encrypt those blocks into fixed-length ciphers. Because the blocks are of a fixed length, keys can be re-used, making key management a breeze.

Streams = bit by bit; block = encrypted in equal sections
Stream = hardware driven; block = software driven
Block = slower encryption; stream = fast encryption

What is SATAN?

SATAN (Security Administrator Tool for Analyzing Networks)
is a security tool designed by Dan Farmer and Wieste Venema to
help systems administrators recognize several network-related security problems.

What are the Types of IT securities you have experienced with?

   I. **Data Integrity**
  II. **Availability**
 III. **Consistency**
 IV. **Control**
  V. **Audit**

Why clipping levels are used?

Clipping levels enable the security administrator to customize the audit trail to record only actions for users with access to user codes with a privileged status.

Have you used the Crossover Error Rate (CER)?

Crossover Error Rate (CER) is a comparison metric for different biometric devices and technologies.

Have you worked with One Time Passwords – Tools?

OPIE is based on S/Key, that contains a seed value, which is a fixed number for each account, and a sequence number, Key features incude RFC 1938 compliance, MD4, MD5 and SHA-1 support, and it's compatible with S/KEY and OPIE.

Explain masquerading?

Spoofing, otherwise known as masquerading, involves the attacker posing as a legitimate network host or application tricking the victim into revealing information.

Explain PDRR?

Prevention, Detection, Response and Recovery

What is information security AIC triad?

Availability, integrity, and confidentiality.

Whats your experience with nonrepudiation?

It is a means to ensure that a transferred message has been sent and received by the parties claiming to have sent and received the message.

Non-repudiation is a property of the transaction that positively confirms that a particular client did indeed request the transaction in question without having the ability to deny making the request.

In e-commerce it is vital.

In my view six security needs in E-commerce are:
   I.   Access Control.
   II. Privacy/Confidentiality.
   III. Authentication.
   IV. Non Repudiation.
   V.   Integrity.
   VI. Availability.

With Pretty Good Privacy (PGP) what can be encrypted?

In my view Pretty Good Privacy (PGP) is a data encryption and decryption computer program that provides cryptographic privacy and authentication for data communication.

PGP is often used for signing, encrypting and decrypting texts, E-mails, files, directories and whole disk partitions to increase the security of e-mail communicate.

In addition to protecting data in transit over a network, PGP encryption can also be used to protect data in long-term data storage.

What is audit trail?

An audit trail (or audit log) is a security-relevant chronological record, set of records, or destination and source of records that provide documentary evidence of the sequence of activities that have affected at any time a specific operation, procedure, or event.

What are the four major components of the threat assessment?

I. Type
II. Mechanism
III. Impact
IV. Probability ALE – Annual Loss Expectancy

Explain Single Sign-On (SSO)?

Single Sign-On (SSO) overcomes the problems of having to log on multiple times to access different network resources. Single Sign-On (SSO) options include: KryptoKnight, Kerberos, and SESAME. Kerberos, SESAME, KryptoKnight, and NetSP are authentication server systems with operational modes that can implement SSO.

Have you used symmetric key cryptography?

Kerberos authenticates clients to other entities on a network of which a client requires services by using a system of symmetric key cryptography.

Its also called secret key cryptography, it relies on a shared secret.

The entity that encrypts the plain text and the entity that decrypts the plain text both must know the key.

The two parties can arrange to exchange the key in some different way, sometimes called OOB for "Out of Bounds".

What is MOM and how it relates to insiders?

"MOM," which stands for: motive, opportunity and means. Insiders have the means and opportunity to launch an attack.

What methods can be used to prevent collusion?

    I. Least Privilege
   II. Mandatory Vacations
  III. Job Rotation
  IV. Separation of Duties

How many phases are in system life cycle?

The system life cycle is typically broken into five phases: initiation, development/acquisition, implementation, operation/maintenance, and disposal.

How you calculate the risk?

Threats * Vulnerability * Asset Value = Total Risk

What is Residual risk?

Residual risk is the amount of risk remaining after security controls have been applied.

Explain Security Through Penetration Testing?

Security through Penetration Testing introduces tools and an overall methodology for penetration testing that can be broken into a three-step process:

I.   Network enumeration - discovering as much as possible about the target.
II. Vulnerability analysis - identifying all potential avenues of attack.
III. Exploitation - attempting to compromise the network by leveraging the results of the vulnerability analysis and following as many avenues identified as time allows.

What is TCSEC Security Book?

Orange Book
What is TCSEC Mandatory Security Policy?

Enforces Access Control Rules based on individual clearance, authorization and confidentiality level of the information

What are TCSEC two types of assurances?

Assurance Mechanisms and Continuous Protection Assurance

What TCSEC four divisions have you worked on?

Trusted Computer Security Evaluation
Criteria (TCSEC) is also called "Orange Book" and it has
Four divisions:
D. C. B. and A.
A are highest and D is lowest.
Levels of trust vary at each division

What is a Covert channel?

A covert channel is any method of communication that is used
to illicitly transfer information, thus breaking the security
policy of the system

What are the types of covert channels you have worked on?

I. **Storage Channels**

Covert storage channels are methods of communication
that "include all vehicles that would allow the direct or
indirect writing of a storage location by one process and
the direct or indirect reading of it by another

II. **Timing Channels**

Covert timing channels are methods of communication that
"include all vehicles that would allow one process to signal
information to another process by modulating its own use of
system resources in such a way that the change in response
time observed by the second process would provide
information"

Define Threat?

The likelihood that a security event will happen in a given time span or the rate.
Security Event Rate (per month, hour etc.)
Name a few network threats?

    I. Information gathering
   II. Sniffing
  III. Spoofing
  IV. Session hijacking
   V. Denial of service

What is Cross Site Request Forgery?

CSRF is an attack which forces an end user to execute unwanted actions on a web application in which he/she is currently authenticated is an attack which forces an end user to execute unwanted actions on a web application in which he/she is currently authenticated.
What solution you propose for CSRF attack?

Use Synchronizer Token Pattern

What port is used by PING?

No ports required for Ping as it uses icmp packets

What are the most important Elements of the Security Life Cycle?

I. Perimeter Protection
II. Risk and Vulnerability Assessment
III. Information Systems Security Policies
IV. Penetration Testing
V. Intrusion Detection

What is a World Wide Name (WWN)?

A World Wide Name, or WWN, is a 64-bit address used in fibre channel networks to uniquely identify each element in a Fibre Channel network. Soft Zoning utilizes World Wide Names to assign security permissions.

The use of World Wide Names for security purposes is inherently insecure, because the World Wide Name of a device is a user-configurable parameter.

For example, to change the World Wide Name (WWN) of an Emulex HBA, the users simply needs to run the `elxcfg` command.

How to you keep updated on network security?

I subscribe to SAN Newsletters SANS NewsBites, Security Alert, ExecuBytes Security news alerts internet storm center, etc. I also read Security Bulletin from all the IT vendors, eg: Microsoft Security Bulletin

What problem you face with cloud based security solutions?

    I. Performance: Excessive latency
   II. Accuracy: Blocking URLs incorrectly

How will you find and infected machine?

I will use a Security Analytics Platform

How will you design an IT security solution for high HTTP/HTTPS traffic?

I will distribute applications and services in and throughout network

What is FCAP (Fibre Channel Authentication Protocol)?

FCAP is an optional authentication mechanism employed between any two devices or entities on a Fibre Channel network using certificates or optional keys.

What are the CHAP security levels?

One-way CHAP authentication. With this level of security, only the target authenticates the initiator.

Mutual CHAP authentication. With this level of security, the target and the initiator authenticate each other.

IPsec. With this level of security, all IP packets sent during data transfers are encrypted and authenticated

For SAN Storage Array Secure Administration what you recommend?

I recommend using the Secure CLI.
For example CLARiiON Navisphere Secure CLI interface (naviseccli, Secure Navicli, SecureNavi, etc.)
For SAN Security Explain SAN zoning?

SAN zoning is a method of arranging Fibre Channel devices into logical groups over the physical configuration of the fabric.

SAN zoning may be utilized to implement compartmentalization of data for security purposes.

What are the different Access Controls Types?

    I.   Discretionary Access Control
   II.   Mandatory Access Control
  III.   Role-Based Access Control

Explain Discretionary Access Control (DAC)?

It allows the owner of the resource to specify which subjects can access which resources. Access control is at the discretion of the owner of the object (file, directory, and device).

What is the limitation of DAC?

DAC cannot protect against Trojan horse, Malware, Software bugs and malicious local users.

Explain your experience with MAC?

I have used Mandatory Access Control (MAC) type of access control in which only the administrator manages the access controls.

It is done by restricting access to objects based on fixed security attributes or "labels" assigned to users and to files or other objects.

It is widely used in government and DoD systems.

MAC and DAC are not mutually exclusive, it is used in conjunction.

Explain the use of Access Control List?

It provides most granular access to protected objects.
I have used it to Control flow of packets through routers.
I can use it to Control inbound and outbound traffic on network segment.
It is used with DAC. It Associates users and groups to certain rights to use, read, write, modify or execute objects on the system.
It is not used with MAC.

If RDP is utilized, how will you secure windows?

I will set RDP connection encryption level to high

What authentication protocol you will use for Windows?

NT LAN Manager version 2 (or NTLMv2)

How will you disable unwanted services in UNIX?

/etc/inetd.conf

How will you disable unwanted TCP application?

/etc/tcpip settings

When and how will you remove setuid bits?

   I. When Setuid programs run with the privileges of the file's owner.

  II. I will find them by unix commands :
```
find / -perm -04000 -ls
find / -perm -02000 -ls
```
III. Then I will disable them by unix commands:
     chmod ug-s

In UNIX where will you disable unwanted processes?

/etc/inttab

Explain the CHAP Security?

1. It is a login system that uses the Challenge Handshake Authentication Protocol. CHAP authenticator sends a "challenge" message to the peer.

2. The peer responds by "one-way hash" function.

3. The authenticator checks the response .If the values match, the authentication is acknowledged; otherwise the connection is terminated.

What is used by a Kerberos authentication process?

Key Distribution Center (KDC) is used to authenticate a client and to issue the Kerberos Client/Server Session Ticket.

What is a smurf attack? How to prevent it?

It uses IP spoofing and broadcasting to send a PING to a group of hosts in a network.
When a host is pinged, it if a broadcast is sent to a network, all of the hosts will answer back to the ping by sending back ICMP message traffic information indicating status to the originator. This results of in an overload of the network and the target system.

To prevent your system from being used as a smurf attack platform, I will disable IP-directed broadcast functionality on all routers.

Explain Phage Viruses?

A Phage virus re-writes an executable program with its own code, to delete or destroy every program it infects.

Explain Static NAT? How to secure it?

Static NAT maps an unregistered IP address to a registered IP address on a one-to-one basis.
NAT security is achieved through the use of a firewall.

Explain your experience with DMZ?

I have used Demilitarized Zone to host internet services without sacrificing unauthorized access to its private network.
I have implemented DMZ between the Internet and an internal network. DMZ contains devices accessible to

Internet traffic, such as Web (HTTP) servers, FTP servers, SMTP (e-mail) servers and DNS servers.

Corporate n/w <--------> firewall <-------> DMZ <------> firewall<-------> Internet
         (web servers)

What is defense in depth?

Defense in depth is the coordinated use of multiple security countermeasures.
It simply means having more than one layer of protection .Defense in depth is an information assurance (IA) concept in which multiple layers of security controls (defense) are placed throughout information.

What different types of firewalls are there?

1. Packet Filters
2. Circuit Level Gateways
3. Application Level Gateways
4. Stateful Multilayer Inspection Firewalls

Proxy servers operate at which TCP/IP layer of OSI?

Proxy servers work on the seventh layer (the Application Layer) of the OSI model,

What is the best practice for Patch for IT Security?

It is critical to the security of a system that the most up-to-date patch cluster is installed.

What is a Challenge/Response Login Process?

Challenge/Response is a method of allowing a user to send their credentials (password/username) to a remote server, without sending their password as plain text.

HOW TO AVOID BREAK-INS? WHICH USER ACCOUNTS SHOULD BE REMOVED?

Remove or Disable Unneeded Default Accounts---The default configuration of the OS often includes guest accounts (with and without passwords), administrator or root level accounts, and accounts associated with local and network services.

For UNIX systems, disable the login shell or provide a login shell with NULL functionality.

Which organizations work to settle domain name disputes?

UDRP, WIPO is the leading ICANN-accredited domain name dispute resolution service providers.

What is Secured Linux?

Security-Enhanced Linux (selinux) is a Linux feature that provides a mechanism for supporting access control security policies, selinux has been integrated into version 2.6 series of the Linux kernel.

What are three functional components of RADIUS or TACACS+?

RADIUS is used to provide authentication, authorization, and accounting
The AAA architectural framework defines the use of RADIUS and TACACS+ protocols, the AAA framework to provide the authentication, authorization, and accounting function.

What is most important IT Security policy for Firewall rules?

A risk analysis must be performed before firewall rules can be created. Verify every firewall change against compliance policies and change requests.

What is most prevalent vector for malware infections? How to

Protect?

E-mail has become the most prevalent vector for malware infections, AV software that is specifically made for running on your e-mail server, gateway SMTP systems that are dedicated to scanning before passing the messages to your e-mail servers, or AV and malware services that are provided by e-mail provider outside of internal network.

How to prevent new virus and worm outbreaks?

Install file attachment filtering at the network perimeter.

Explain a perimeter-based solution that can block email threats including spam, viruses, and worms?

The network-perimeter protection, the McAfee®SaaS Email Protection service.

Its perimeter-based solution that blocks email threats including spam, viruses, worms and harmful content and attachments.

How to check if anti-virus scanner is working?

EICAR allows users to check whether their antivirus software is running.

What is Microsoft Word's macro virus protection tool, and how do I activate it?

If you are unable to save a document in Microsoft Word, your computer may have a macro virus. Microsoft Word documents can use macros, which can potentially carry these viruses. To minimize this possibility, activate the built-in macro protection tool.

What is the advantage of Security tokens?

Security tokens provide an extra level of assurance through a method known as two-factor authentication: the user has a personal identification number (PIN).

 Access to secured files and data requires both the device and the PIN.

Describe NTLM? How it authenticates?

In a Windows network, NTLM (NT LAN Manager) is a suite of Microsoft security protocols that provides authentication, integrity, and confidentiality to users.
The LANMAN challenge/response and NTLMv1 protocols authenticate users in the following manner:

  I. Client sends an authentication request to the Server.
  II. A protocol negotiation occurs between the Client and Server.
  III. The Server sends the Client a (pseudo-random) 8-byte challenge.
  IV. The Client sends a 24-byte response.
  V. The Server authenticates the Client.

How Screening Router works?

It Filters traffic passing between one network and another with two interfaces—external and internal—each with its own unique IP address, Performs IP forwarding, based on an access control list (ACL).

Can you propose a solution for a stateful packet filtering?

Yes, I will implement two routers, one firewall,
Router positioned on the outside will perform initial, static packet filtering
Router positioned just inside the network will route traffic to appropriate computers in stateful packet filtering

What is Reverse Firewall? How it enhances security?

Reverse firewall inspects ,monitors traffic going out of a network rather than trying to block what's coming in , helps block distributed denial of service (ddos) attacks, can be installed in external and/or internal routers at the perimeter of the network.

How to protect password token?

By using a personal identification number

What is OTP security?

ONE TIME PASSWORD SECURITY.

The OPT device creates a 2 factor security system which means user will have to know something (user name, password and pin) and have something (the otp security token) in order to login into your account.
One-time passwords (OTP) are a good alternative to static passwords. A keyless token security token doesn't have any particular key or identification number innately.

What happens when when multiple administrators share access to a single privileged account?

When multiple administrators share access to a single privileged account, it is impossible to associate administrative changes with the people who initiated them.

This lack of accountability may violate internal control requirements.

In a windows Web server, that has two network interfaces how prevent routing between them?

Turning off IP forwarding prevents packets from being forwarded from one network to another network through this system.

Is it possible to recover passwords via brute force password attacks?

L0phtcrack can brute-force the hashes taken from network logs or programs like pwdump and recover the plaintext password.

What is Port 31337? How to Secure Port 31337?

Port 31337 uses the udp protocol for service type BackOrifice.A malformed request to port 31337 is known to cause denial of service attacks. By default, the firewall should disallow traffic to port 31337 until all security checks have been passed.

What is the most efficient filtering method in least time?

Access Control Lists on border routers.
Border routers are used to provide security between the Internet and the LAN; the router access control lists enforce specific security or business requirements.

When assigning system privileges, which categorization provides the greatest

Flexibility for security administration?

Roles the individual plays in the organization.

In computer systems security, role-based access control (RBAC) is an approach to restricting system access to authorized users. It is used by the majority of enterprises and can be implemented via mandatory access control (MAC) or discretionary access control (DAC). RBAC is sometimes referred to as role-based security.

Which network protocol provides system availability information?

ICMP

Monitor computer availability with ICMP Ping, it checks a remote host for availability.

What is the Principle of Default Deny?

When the Principle of Default Deny has been implemented, anything that is not explicitly allowed is denied regardless of whether the function is related to access, privileges, some security-related attribute or other similar function.

How to Protect Data that is accessed via PC Desktop?

Password protected screen savers with timeouts should be installed on desktops, screen savers used on the computer should be password protected.

Which procedures are critical to maintaining secure configuration and effective security policy?

Maintaining the secure configuration through application of appropriate patches and upgrades, security testing, monitoring of logs, and backups of data.
This model places importance on raising awareness of IT security threats and risks, and associated consequences of IT security-related behavior and actions

What is NIDS?

A Network Intrusion Detection System (NIDS) is an intrusion detection system that tries to detect malicious activity such as denial of service attacks, port scans or even attempts to crack into computers by Network Security Monitoring (NSM) of network traffic.

A NIDS is not limited to inspecting incoming network traffic only it can be used on the inside or outside of the corporate network.

If a Crime contain a digital signature what should be done with the computer that was hacked?

Send it to Computer Forensics experts who will image, protect and preserve the evidence

In Computer Forensics which data they are concerned with?

There are three types of data: active, archival, and latent.

What is a Digital ID?

A Digital ID, sometimes called a digital certificate, is a file on your computer that identifies who you are.

What make A Digital ID?

It typically contains the following information:
  I.   Your public key
  II. Your name and e-mail address
  III. Expiration date of the public key
  IV. Name of the company (the Certification Authority (CA)) who issued your Digital ID
  V.   Serial number of the Digital ID
  VI. Digital signature of the CA

What is public key infrastructure (PKI)? Give an example.

PKI describes a system that uses public keys and Digital IDs to ensure security of the system and to confirm the identity of its users. For example, a company might use PKI to control that accesses the company's computer network.

What is a hash algorithm? Give some examples.

A hash function is a math equation that uses text (such as an e-mail message) to create a code called a message digest. Examples of hash functions are MD4, MD5, and SHS.

What is a message digest?

A message digest is the results you get when you run text (such as an e-mail message)
Through a hash algorithm.

Who is responsible for installing the security patch?

It is the customer's responsibility to install the security patch.

What kind of rights you will allow for server services or all services?

Server services should have lowest possible user rights.

What does your digital certificate represents? How to protect?

Your personal identity, you should protect your private key by token and pass phrase

Certificates are authenticated, issued by whom?

Certificates are authenticated, issued, and managed by a trusted third party called a certification authority (CA)

How to verify the digital signature of the Issuing Authority?

A root certificate is the digital certificate of an Issuing Authority. The public key in this certificate is used to verify the digital signature of the Issuing Authority.

When and why to use Professional accounting and audit firms?

Audit accuracy and reliability of corporate certificate Authority's Issuance policy.

How many ways and a firewall management program can be configured?

A firewall management program can be configured one of two basic ways:

    I. A default-deny policy. The firewall administrator lists the allowed network services, and everything else is denied.

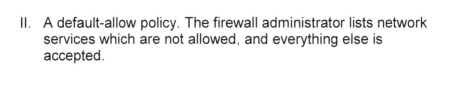

II. A default-allow policy. The firewall administrator lists network services which are not allowed, and everything else is accepted.

What is the only way to guard against application layer attacks?

Application-level proxy

Which command will show you which ports are open or in use?

On Unix Netstat command will show you whatever ports are open or in use.

On Windows the netstat.exe command can help you with basic networking issues, such as what ports are active on your personal computer, troubleshooting network connectivity problems.

Why Security patches should be installed immediately?

The risks a business is exposed to by security vulnerabilities and the associated costs of security breaches against unpatched systems are greater.

What is IKE?

The IKE protocol is a key management protocol standard .ISAKMP, Oakley, and Skeme are security protocols implemented by IKE.

What are symmetric key cryptographic algorithms? Why you need them?

For securing data with symmetric encryption (DES, AES (Rijndael), RC5, CAST IDEA

What is the use of Message digest functions? Which are commonly used?

Message digest functions also called hash functions, are used to produce digital summaries of information called message digests.

Two of the most commonly used message digest algorithms today are MD5, a 128-bit digest developed by RSA Data Security, Inc., and SHA-1, a 160-bit message digest developed by the National Security Agency.

From where the encryption algorithm is inherited? What are the classes?

The encryption algorithm is inherited from the global default policy and can be overridden at the client level.

There are 3 classes of hosts that need differing types and amount of encryption:
Developers
Payroll
CEO

What is Transport Agent?

Transport Agent mail program that functions behind the scenes to ensure that messages are transported in an orderly fashion according to SMTP protocol daemon
Transport agent's saves mail in a mailbox.

How to prevent a single point of failure in security mechanisms?

To eliminate single points of failure and to maximize performance, a fully distributed security model needs to combine the benefits of centralized control with distributed and parallel methods.

How can you implement synergistic security?

I will install firewall in series with a screening router for defense in depth. .
The Firewall and Screening Router work in tandem ensuring that only authorized request are allowed to reach the Web Server.

What is an acceptable use policy?

Acceptable use policy governs the use of computers and networks.

Explain PoLP?

The principle of least privilege
The principle of least privilege PoLP.
It's also known as the principle of least authority.
It is an important concept in computer security.
Minimal user profile privileges on computers based on users' job necessities.

What you should do if you received a virus warning from your friend?

Don't trust anything that does not come directly from an information technology professional.

I will not do anything until I have verified the "warning" through a credible source, such as: The computer Virus Myths web site

What is STO?

Security through Obscurity (STO) is the belief that a system of any sort can be secure so long as nobody outside of its implementation group is allowed to find out anything about its internal mechanisms.

What are recommended Ed Synergistic Controls at the Desktop-Level?

I. Enable Macro Virus Protection in Microsoft Office© Programs

II. Use the anti-virus software heuristic controls (in full-time background mode where available)

III. Synergistic Controls at the E-Mail Client Level

IV. Turn off auto-open attachments

V. Configure email clients to convert email messages to "plain text" format

VI. Configure to block execution of all executable attachments as well as other attachments known to pose a security risk.

VII. Executable attachments e.g.: *.EXE, *.HTA, *.VBS, etc.

VIII. Configure to challenge opening of other attachments that could pose a security risk.

IX. Configure to challenge double click of all attachments

Why you need Access Lists?

Access lists filter network traffic by controlling whether routed packets are forwarded or blocked at the router's interfaces.

What is the use of Digital Signatures?

Digital Signatures is the electronic equivalent of a physical signature and can be used to electronically sign any document or transaction.

What problems have you noticed with FTP?

FTP utilizes a dynamic secondary port for data channels

What kind of security issue you have dealt with in NIS?

Any machine within an NIS domain can use commands to extract information from the server without authentication.

What is DNS cache poisoning?

A False IP with a high time-to-live will stay in the cache of The DNS server for a long time.

DNS cache poisoning (sometimes referred to as cache pollution) is an attack technique that allows an attacker to introduce forged DNS information into the cache of a caching name server.

What is Website crawling? Is it and an attack?

Web crawler is a script that scans Internet pages to create an index of data.
Also called a bot, web crawlers but it's not an attack.

Why to protect your website from a Crawler?

Website crawling robots drastically eats up a website's bandwidth unnecessarily.

For what is IMAP used?

IMAP (Internet Message Access Protocol) is a network protocol used to access e-mail messages while they are still stored on the server.

What is FTP, In terms of security what makes it difficult to control the File Transfer Protocol (FTP) via a firewall rule set or packet filter?

FTP is a TCP based service exclusively. There are two channels; one for commands and one for data .There is no UDP component to FTP. FTP is an unusual service in that it utilizes two ports, a 'data' port and a 'command' port (also known as the control port). Traditionally these are port 21 for the command port and port 20 for the data port. The confusion begins however, when we find that depending on the mode, the data port is not always on port 20.

Explain your experience with DNS, and what you did to make it secure?

The Domain Name System (DNS) is used for resolving host names into Internet Protocol (IP) addresses. Insecure underlying protocols and lack of authentication and integrity checking of the information within the DNS threatens the proper functionality of the DNS. That's why they came up with DNSSEC.DNSSEC is an addition to the Domain Name System (DNS) protocols.DNSSEC allows for a DNS zone and all the records in the zone to be cryptographically signed.

How does DNSSec provide greater security?

It supports cryptographically signed zones for greater trust across the domain name
System.

What are the tasks associated with DNSSEC?

Doing DNSSEC involves two tasks:

   I. Cryptographically signing authoritative DNS records, and

   II. Validating those signatures on recursive resolvers.

What is SMTP, Which port it runs? Explain How to make it secure?

SIMPLE MAIL TRANSFER PROTOCOL (SMTP) is an Internet standard for electronic mail (e-mail) transmission across Internet Protocol (IP) networks. Port 25.

To Make it secure I had used SMTP Security Options:

Reject mail if sender address is from an invalid domain

Authenticated senders must use valid sender address
Senders from local domains must authenticate to send email
Hide IP addresses from email headers

When to use Tripwire?

Open Source Tripwire is a free software security and data integrity tool useful for monitoring and alerting on specific file change(s) on a range of systems.
Open Source Tripwire functions as a host-based intrusion detection system.
Detect changes in a file without storing the entire contents of the file in the database.

You have to save storage and backup data with security, how you can do it?

I will first compress and then encrypt the data.

What is a bonnet?

BOTNET IS A LARGE NUMBER OF COMPROMISED COMPUTERS THAT ARE USED TO GENERATE SPAM. BOT IS SHORT FOR ROBOT. CRIMINALS USE BOTNET TO DISTRIBUTE MALICIOUS SOFTWARE THAT CAN TURN YOUR COMPUTER INTO A BOT.

What security features you should look for in software?

User Passwords encrypted
Account Lockout
Session Timeout

Sensitive Data Encryption

Tell us what you know about web intrusion detection system?

Intrusion Detection Systems are like a burglar alarm for your computer network. Web applications read all types of input from users. Web intrusion detection contains SSL; HTTP protocol; logging; alert mechanism for Web based applications.

Vulnerable web servers can be to attacks over port 80, the default TCP/IP port used for HTTP traffic. Secure Sockets Layer (SSL) is a protocol for encrypting data between the end user's browser and a web serve; it acts when malicious activities are detected according to rules generated from the frequency of accesses and characteristics of HTTP traffic.

What is Cross site scripting?

Cross-site scripting (XSS) is a type of computer security vulnerability typically found in Web applications that enables attackers to inject client-side script into Web pages viewed by other users. Web Browsers execute codes like JavaScript, Flash and many other codes and an attacker could get to that website to forward the attack.

Can HTTP handle state?

HTTP cannot handle states. It uses cookies to handle the state.

What key will you use for encryption and which one will you use for signing?

Use different keys for encryption and signing

WHAT TYPE OF HOME NETWORK DO YOU USE?

WIRELESS, PERSONAL AREA NETWORK, LOCAL AREA NETWORK, AND VIRTUAL PRIVATE NETWORK.

What are TCP Infrastructure attacks?

It's by TCP sequence guessing, because TCP connections rely on an increasing
sequence number to correctly order traffic over connection ,If an attacker knows the sequence numbers of a connection stream he can generate correct-looking packets
For example rsh command.

How to secure a router?

Disable wireless administrating. Turn Off the setting that allows administrating the router through a wireless connection. Serial Connection is the most secure means of administering a router.

What ports are echo service and chargen?

Echo service (port 7) and chargen (port 19)

What is the purpose of chargen (port 19)?

Chargen

Chargen is short for Character Generator and is a service that generates random characters either in one UDP packet containing a random number (between 0 and 512) of characters, or a TCP session. The UDP Chargen server looks for a UDP packet on port 19 and responds with the random character packet.

Explain TCP and UDP Small Servers?

TCP and UDP small servers are servers (daemons, in UNIX parlance) that run in the router which are useful for diagnostics.

TCP Small Servers

I. Echo: Echoes back whatever you type through the telnet x.x.x.x echo command.

II. Chargen: Generates a stream of ASCII data. Use the telnet x.x.x.x chargen command.

III. Discard: Throws away whatever you type. Uses the telnet x.x.x.x discard command.

IV. Daytime: Returns system date and time, if it is correct. It is correct if you run Network Time Protocol (NTP), or have set the date and time manually from the exec level. Use the telnet x.x.x.x daytime command.

Explain UDP Small Servers?

The UDP small servers are:

Echo: Echoes the payload of the datagram you send.

Discard: Silently pitches the datagram you send.

Chargen: Pitches the datagram you send, and responds with a 72-character string of ASCII characters terminated with a CR+LF.

What is SOCKS?

It is a generic proxy protocol for TCP/IP-based networking

What is Belt and Suspenders?

Belt and Suspenders approach uses layers of security are making it more dependable.
To guard against single points of failure, the "Belt and Suspenders" Approach to security installs redundant layers of security to the System. The idea being that if your belt gives way, the suspenders are still there to hold your pants up.

What are two uses of the TCP wrappers package?

The TCP Wrappers package (tcp_wrappers) is installed by default and provides host-based access control to network services.

When a connection attempt is made to a TCP-wrapped service, the service first references the host's access files (/etc/hosts. allow and /etc/hosts. deny) to determine whether or not the client is allowed to connect.

In most cases, it then uses the syslog daemon (syslogd) to write the name of the requesting client and the requested service to /var/log/secure or /var/log/messages.

What is Network address translation (NAT)? When to use it?

Network address translation (NAT) takes IP addresses used on one network and translates them into IP addresses used within another network.
You use NAT to hide network addresses from hosts on another network.

What is defense in depth?

Defense in depth is an information assurance (IA) concept in which multiple layers of security controls (defense) are placed throughout information. Defense in depth is the coordinated use of multiple security countermeasures.

Proxy servers operate at which TCP/IP layer?

Proxy servers work on the seventh layer (the Application Layer) of the OSI model,

What is the best practice for Paching OS?

It is critical to the security of a system that the most up-to-date patch cluster is installed.

What is a Challenge/Response Login Process?

Challenge/Response is a method of allowing a user to send their credentials (password/username) to a remote server, without sending their password as plain text.

How to to avoid security break-ins on user accounts on internet servers?

Disable all general user accounts
Remove or Disable Un needed Default Accounts, guest accounts, severely restrict access to the accounts, including changing the names.
Disable Non-Interactive Accounts
For UNIX systems, disable the login shell or provide a login shell with NULL functionality (e.g., /bin/false).

How to manage software licenses?

Technology Security and Compliance department should be responsible to manages software license agreements and review all software licenses.

Which organizations work to settle domain name disputes?

 UDRP, WIPO is the leading ICANN-accredited domain name dispute resolution service
Providers.

What is SELinux?

Security-Enhanced Linux (SELinux) is a Linux feature that provides a mechanism for supporting access control security policies, SELinux has been integrated into version 2.6 series of the Linux kernel.

Why RADIUS is used?

RADIUS is used to provide authentication, authorization, and accounting
The AAA architectural framework defines the use of RADIUS and TACACS+ protocols; the AAA framework is used to provide the authentication, authorization, and accounting function.

What is the best practice for making Changes to the firewall

configuration?

A risk analysis must be performed before firewall rules can be created. Verify every firewall change against compliance policies and change requests.

What is the most prevalent vector for company-wide infection? How to prevent it?

E-mail and browser-based personal mail service has become the most prevalent vector for malware infections. By implementing gateway, or network edge, protection where files are filtered at the mail gateway in preventing problems from cropping up.

For example:
The McAfee SaaS Email Protection service is a comprehensive, perimeter-based solution that blocks over 99 percent of email threats including spam, viruses, worms and harmful content and attachments – before they can enter and damage internal messaging networks.

What security rule you have for Dial-in modems?

Disable maintenance modems or require strong authentication before allowing remote maintenance. Block unauthorized traffic on the phone system.

Which file type you should never open?

Never open up file attachments ending with ".exe" ".vbs" ".bat" ".com" ".scr" and ".pif" without confirming with the sender, they may contain virus.

The ".vbs" file extension should always be treated with suspicion. VBS stands for "visual basic script".

Which international organization provides copyright law?

The World Intellectual Property Organization Copyright Treaty, abbreviated as the WIPO Copyright Treaty, is an international treaty on copyright law adopted by the member states of the World Intellectual Property Organization (WIPO) in 1996. It provides additional protections for copyright.

Whats your view about reusable password?

Any reusable password is subject to eavesdropping attacks from sniffer programs

What is Hash?

Hash is a special form of encryption often used for passwords that uses a one-way algorithm that when provided with a variable length unique input (message) will always provide a unique fixed length unique output called hash, or message digest.

Name 2 most used cryptographic hash functions?

MD5 and SHA-1.

Have you used ESP? Why?

Encapsulating Security Payloads (ESP) provide confidentiality, data origin .ESP also supports encryption-only and authentication-only configurations
With Encapsulating Security Payload (ESP), traffic is typically encrypted using Data Encryption Standard (DES) or Triple DES (3DES) and authenticated with SHA1 or MD5.

How to defending an enterprise network against internal threats?

Deploy 'intrawalls' firewalls between departments.

Can you propose solutions that offer full protection in defending an enterprise network against external threats?

Brocade NetIron MLX switches to defend large enterprise network cores against external threats.

McAfee's network access control, intrusion prevention, and firewall solutions, with Brocade Ironview Network Manager through open standards network management protocols.

What is one use of firewalls?

Firewalls can block attackers from communicating with your system, so they cannot attack it.

Whats your recommendation on Firewalls?

The hardware firewalls offer faster response times, and hence handle more traffic loads.
It has its own operating system so it is less prone for attacks

WHAT IS THE MOST COMMON FORM OF SECURITY

VULNERABILITY?

Buffer overflows

What do digital certificates used to exchange to get public key?

Digital signatures need to use digital certificates to obtain the needed public key

In which X.509 certificate handling and processing defined?

ISO/IEC/ITU 9594-8
Name two methods used by Entrust/PKI to extend trust between Certification

Authorities (CAs)?

Peer-to-peer cross-certification and hierarchical cross-certification.

Which is a step in system hardening?

Some basic hardening techniques are as follows:

I. Non-essential services
II. Patches and Fixes
III. Password Management
IV. Unnecessary accounts
V. File and Directory Protection use of Access Control Lists (ACLs)
VI. File and File System Encryption
VII. Enable Logging
VIII. File Sharing

Distributed Denial of Service Attacks

What is one of the most common avenues of attack used for system break-ins?

The most common and obvious type of DoS attack occurs when an attacker "floods" a network with information.

What is a denial-of-service (DoS) attack?

In a denial-of-service (DoS) attack, an attacker attempts to prevent legitimate users from accessing information or services.

What is Grayware?

It encompasses spyware, adware, dialers, joke programs, remote access tools, and any other unwelcome files and programs apart from viruses that are designed to harm the performance of computers on your network.

Grayware refers to applications or files that are not classified as viruses or Trojan horse programs, but can still negatively affect the performance of the computers on your network and introduce significant security risks to your organization.

Grayware performs a variety of undesired actions such as irritating users with pop-up windows, tracking user habits and unnecessarily exposing computer vulnerabilities to attack.

What is the primary mechanism for a malicious code to enter a desktop?

E-Mail Attachments

What is a data warehouse?

A data warehouse is a duplicate of some or all of a main database's data stored on a separate computer from the main database its a collection of data designed to support management decision making.

What is the default cipher for the IPSec?

Data Encryption Standard (DES) algorithm in the Cipher Block Chaining (CBC)

What is the difference between clearing and purging information?

Clearing information is a level of media sanitization that would protect the confidentiality of information against a robust keyboard attack.
PURGING INFORMATION is a media sanitization process that protects the confidentiality of *INFORMATION* against a laboratory attack.

Name encryption software implementations?

PGP, SSL, Kerberos

What problems you have seen in Kerberos implementation?

The problem is that Key Distribution Center server (KDC) uses a global variable for all incoming krb4 requests but sets the variable only for certain requests. This can be exploited to crash an affected server, potentially execute arbitrary code, or disclose potentially sensitive memory.

The MIT krb5 Kerberos implementation includes a GSS RPC library used in the Kerberos administration server (kadmind). Two flaws exist in the libgssprc library that can cause an array overrun if too many file descriptors are opened. These flaws result in a vulnerability that could allow memory corruption in the kadmind server.

Secure Socket Layer works at which TCP/IP Layer?

Transport

When is DES required?

Getting kerberos to work

What are 3 Types of encryption?

    I. Symmetric
   II. Asymmetric
  III. Hash

When VPNs should be used?

Only for emails.

What steps you will take to secure your wireless LAN?

I will use strong encryption
I will modify the default ssid
I will deploy mutual authentication
I will secure the wire line

What happens in social engineering attack?

In a social engineering attack, an attacker uses human interaction i.e. social skills to obtain or compromise information about an organization or its computer systems.

The Hacker tricks a company's employee into revealing passwords or critical information that may be used to compromise security.

How to avoid social engineering and phishing attacks?

Do not give sensitive information to anyone unless you are sure that they are indeed who they claim to be and that they should have access to the information.

How to stop buffer overflow vulnerabilities?

Buffer overflow vulnerabilities are caused by programming errors that allow an attacker to cause the program to write beyond the bounds of an allocated memory, by quality coding practices it can be avoided.

What is Cold Spare in Disaster recovery?

Cold Spare is a System intended for use in the event of a disaster, shutdown or failure of the primary. A Cold Spare is not used in production but is available to expedite recovery time.

What are Honey pots?

Honey pot system is used to deceive intruders and learn from them, their tools and methods without compromising the security of the network.

How to provide security by Host-Based Intrusion Prevention

Systems (HIPSs)?

Most HIPSs work by sand-boxing by restricting the definition of acceptable behavior rules .The prevention occurs at the agent residing at the host. The agent intercepts system calls or system messages by utilizing dynamic linked libraries (dll) substitution.

How Intrusion detection systems are classified? Types?

By monitoring scope.
Network-based intrusion detection and host-based detections.

How LFM provides Security?

Log File Monitors (LFM)

LFMs creates a record of log files generated by network services and monitors this record for system trends, tendencies, and patterns in the log files that would suggest an intruder is attacking.

How to find the chain of custody for Computer related issues?

The evidence log provides a log that details the chain of custody. This is used to describe who had possession of the evidence.

What a Security incident response procedure document contains?

Security incident response team roles, as well as how to define a security incident response plan.

What is penetration testing?

The penetration testing can be broken into a three-step process:

I. Network enumeration: Discover as much as possible about the target.
II. Vulnerability analysis: Identify all potential avenues of attack.
III. Exploitation: Attempt to compromise the network

Why and How to perform the Penetration Testing for Web Applications?

It is an audit service intended to detect potential known security vulnerabilities in corporate resources (web applications, ftp, e-mail, web, firewall, etc.) before attackers can discover them.
Steps:

I. Exploration Phase
II. Automatic Security Scanning
III. Manual Check Phase
IV. Reporting
V. Verification Phase

What to monitor in employee internet usage?

I. Internet sites accessed by the employees
II. Protocols used by them for communication.
III. Non-Business Hour web usage details and trends.
IV. Internet abuse and excessive internet usage.
V. Tab of employee internet transactions that can cause attacks & virus
VI. Restricted sites like streaming and chat sites.

How many backups needed for best protection against data loss?

At least three copies of your data:

I. The original files
II. An easily-accessible backup and
III. A protected copy of your backup

What are the security standards for Merchants accepting Credit Cards?

    I. All merchants, regardless if credit card data is stored, must achieve and maintain compliance at all times (all deadlines have passed);

    II. Merchants cannot store certain credit card information including cvv2, cvc2 and cid codes (three or four-digit numbers), track data from the magnetic strip or pin data;

    III. If permitted credit card information such as name, credit card number and expiration date is stored, certain security standards are required.

Name a few security requirements for Cloud?

    I. Identifying and authenticating users
    II. Secure vendor relationships
    III. Prevent external attacks
    IV. Encrypt information

Name a few security technologies that can be used for cloud computing environment?

    I. Firewalls
    II. Anti-virus and anti-malware
    III. Encryption for data in motion
    IV. Patch management
    V. Log management

What is PCI DSS?

The Payment Card Industry Data Security Standard (PCI DSS)

It's a comprehensive security standard that establishes common processes and precautions for handling, processing, storing and transmitting credit card data.

Payment Card Industry Data Security Standard (PCI DSS) has 12 mandated security requirements:

Install and maintain a firewall configuration to protect data
do not use default passwords and other security parameters
Protect stored data
Encrypt transmission of cardholder data and sensitive information
Use and regularly update anti-virus software
Develop and maintain secure systems and applications
Restrict access to data by business need-to-know
Assign a unique ID to each person with computer access
Restrict physical access to cardholder data
Track and monitor all access to network resources and cardholder data
Regularly test security systems and processes
Maintain a policy that addresses information security
Reference: PCI DSS

Which are popular Email Ports?

POP3 - port 110
IMAP - port 143
SMTP - port 25
HTTP - port 80
Secure SMTP (SSMTP) - port 465
Secure IMAP (IMAP4-SSL) - port 585
IMAP4 over SSL (IMAPS) - port 993
Secure POP3 (SSL-POP) - port 995

Explain your experience with SSL? What are security levels?

SSL encryption protects data during transmission.
Securing remote transmissions using SSL.

Web servers and Web browsers rely on the Secure Sockets Layer (SSL) protocol to create a uniquely **encrypted** channel for private communications over the public Internet. Each SSL Certificate consists of a **public key and a private key**.

Possible Security Levels Are:
    Level 3 (SECURE)
    Level 2 (ANY)
    Level 1 (NONSECURE)

Explain the use of TCP Wrappers?

TCP Wrappers can be used to GRANT or DENY access to various Services.

Explain your experience with the RPC Mapper? What Kind of attack happens on RPC?

The *PORT MAPPER* program maps Remote Procedure Call *(RPC)* Program and version numbers to transport-specific *PORT* numbers. The port mapper (rpc.portmap or just portmap, or rpcbind) is an ONC RPC service.
The port mapper service always uses TCP or UDP port 111;

Microsoft RPC end-point-mapper runs on port 135 .A remote attackers could send a specially-crafted request to the RPC Endpoint Mapper service on port 135 to cause all RPC services to fail.

Explain your experience with Java Security issues?

I have come across this issue where an error in the Java Runtime Environment Virtual Machine can be exploited by a malicious, untrusted applet to read and write local files and execute local applications.

How to avoid Brute – force attacks?

The most effective way to block brute-force attacks is to simply lock out accounts after a defined number of incorrect passwords.

Explain your experience with Apache vulnerabilities?

Apache HTTP Server contains a buffer overflow in the mod_proxy module; The Apache Server uses the mod_proxy module to implement proxying for various common protocols such as FTP and HTTP.

Explain OpenSSH Signal Handling Vulnerability?

Signal handler race condition in OpenSSH versions below 4.4 allows remote attackers to cause a denial of service (crash) and possibly execute arbitrary code if Generic Security Services Application Program Interface (GSSAPI) authentication is enabled using unspecified vectors.

What is Zero-Day attacks?

Zero-Day attacks are attacks on vulnerabilities that have not been patched or made public, while others define them as attacks that take advantage of security vulnerability on the same day that the vulnerability becomes publicly known (zero-day).

Zero-day attacks target publicly known but still unpatched vulnerabilities.

In terms of Security will you use switch or a hub?

Switch provides security on data, because it directly transfers, while hub broadcast data.

What is Filtering?

Filters allow or block packets.

How does a packet filter work?

Operating at the network layer and transport layer of the TCP/IP protocol stack, every packet is examined by filter as it enters the protocol stack.

Name the Types of Filter Techniques?

Packet filtering (routers)
Stateful Packet Filtering
Application Gateway (proxy)

How to make a secure web server?

I will install OS and applications
I will apply all patches
I will remove sample files
I will install production code on web server
I will test
I will use secure connection to Internet

How to calculate Risk related to IT Security?

Risk = *THREAT x VULNERABILITY x COST*

Explain Port Scan Attack?

Port Scan Attack is one of the most popular reconnaissance techniques attackers uses. By port scanning the attacker finds which ports are available.

What is Point-to-Point Tunneling Protocol (PPTP)? Why not use PPTP?

PPTP is a protocol that allows PPP connections to be tunneled through an IP network, creating a VPN.Point to Point Tunneling Protocol (PPTP) is a network protocol.

It enables the secure transfer of data from a remote client to a private enterprise server by creating a VPN across TCP/IP-based data networks.

PPTP supports on-demand, multiprotocol, virtual private networking over public networks, such as the Internet.

In my view the point to point tunneling protocol (PPTP) is not secure enough, its MSCHAP V2 authentication, it can be broken trivially by capture of the DataStream, and how MPPE depends on the MSCHAP tokens for cryptographic keys. MPPE is also only 128-bit, easy to attack, and the keys used at each end are the same, which lowers the effort required to succeed.

The lack of two-factor authentication, relying on a single username and password, is a risk.

What is the default port for HTTP Service?

Default ports: 80 for HTTP, 443 for HTTPS

Explain your experience with SMB? Is SMB Secure?

Windows clients use Server Message Block, SMB, to share files in local network.
SMB is used in most firms that have any Windows computers, because it is easy to install to Windows. Linux is a popular choice for an SMB server, because it can serve more clients with the same hardware. SMB is completely inherently insecure.
It does not encrypt traffic, so it can only be used in a LAN, relying on company firewall.

Is it possible to crack password that is encrypted?

Password encryption can be bypassed with widely available programs, such as l0pthcrack.

Can Samba Make SMB Secure?

Sharing files on a Windows box opens it to many exploits.

Even though it is a lot harder to crack into a Linux, Samba cannot make SMB secure.

What is spoofing?

    I. To deceive
   II. A hoax

What is the motive behind the Denial of Service attack?

The goal of a denial of service attack is to deny legitimate users access to a particular resource.

Which ports used by Windows are Most Vulnerable?

The ports used by Windows NetBIOS over TCP/IP are among the most vulnerable to hackers.

Which ports NetBIOS uses over TCP?

NetBIOS session traffic over TCP port 139
NetBIOS name management traffic over UDP port 137
NetBIOS datagram traffic over UDP port 138

Explain your experience with a personal firewall?

With a personal firewall protection, the computer is expected to be safe from intrusion from outsiders so that the entire user's personal data is safe.

I will use it to Checks the network traffic of the computer.
It will warn me of any attempt made by a certain application trying to access the Net or the local network, and scans possible malicious software and warns the user if there is any malicious outside program trying to access the computer.

It will immediately act after detecting suspicious behavior, such as tampering the user's computer and hides the computer from automated port scans by blocking unauthorized network traffic.

What you look for in a Firewall?

Distributed Denial of Service protection, traffic management functionality, and firewall throughputs.

What method most firewalls can use to inform an administrator what is going on?

Logging provides me an insight into the firewall.

Logging is the only method most firewalls can use to inform an administrator what is going on.

By collecting and reviewing the firewall logs, an administrator will rapidly learn the normal and abnormal behavior for the firewall, making it much easier to determine when and how to intervene where necessary to correct the situation.

There are two methods of logging:

Syslog logging
Proprietary logging

Explain your experience with Demilitarized Zone (DMZ) for Security?

In an information technology Security context:

Demilitarized Zone (DMZ) =A logical area that resides between the public Internet and an internal private network.

I have used DMZ for Web services or devices that require a public IP address.
Basic networked computers do not reside on the DMZ; they should reside in the protected, private network. Also I use a firewall or a router that usually protects the DMZ with traffic-filtering capabilities, often with the aid of an Intrusion Detection/Prevention Service.

As an it auditor what you know about IOPS?

Max IOPS an HBA Port can generate to any LUN = (Device Queue Depth per LUN * (1 / (Storage Latency in ms/1000)))

Calculation of the maximum Queue Depth: The queue depth is the number of I/O operations that can be run in parallel on a device.
Q = Storage Port Max Queue Depth / (I * L),
Q is the Queue Depth =Execution Throttle= Maximum Number of simultaneous I/O for each LUN any particular path to the Storage Port.

I is the number of initiators per Storage port
L is the quantity of LUNs in the storage group.

Max IOPS an HBA Port can generate to any LUN = (Device Queue Depth per LUN * (1 / (Storage Latency in ms/1000)))

As an it auditor what you know about WWN

A WWNN is a World Wide Node Name; used to uniquely identify a device in a Storage Area Network (SAN).
A WWPN is a World Wide Port Name; a unique identifier for each Fibre Channel port presented to a Storage Area Network (SAN).

WWN FORMATS

    I. Vendor Unique Code
  II. Product Code
 III. Product Type
 IV. Serial Number
  V. Port Number

WWPN FORMATS

    I. Section 1 – Format ID
  II. Section 2 – Vendor ID
 III. Section 3 - Vendor Unique

As an it auditor what you know about FIBRE CHANNEL LAYERS

Fibre channel Layer	Role
I. FC - 4	Defines how a Fibre Channel network will communicate with upper level applications (Audio / Video / IPI / SCSI / HIPPI / IP / 802.2)
II. FC - 3	For advanced features: Striping, Hunt groups, Multicast
III. FC - 2	Similar to the MAC (Media Access Layer) and defines how data from upper level applications is split into frames for transport over the lower layers (Framing Protocol / Flow Control)
IV. FC - 1	Defines how frames are encoded and decoded for transport (Encode / Decode). The information

	transmitted over a fibre is encoded 8 bits at a time into a 10 bit Transmission Character.
V. FC - 0	Defines the various media types that can carry Fibre Channel data (Single, Multimode, Copper: 133Mb, 266Mb, 531Mb, 1.06G, 2.12G & 4.25G)

As an it auditor what you know about EUI - EXTENDED UNIQUE IDENTIFIER FORMAT

The IEEE defined 64-bit extended unique identifier (EUI-64) is a concatenation of a 24-bit Organizationally Unique Identifier (OUI) value administered by the IEEE Registration Authority and a 40-bit extension identifier assigned by the organization with that OUI assignment.

```
N
 A  OUI     VSID
 A
| - | ------- | ----------- |
```

The EUI format takes the form eui.16 hex digits.

As an it auditor what you know about SCSI STANDARDS

I. SCSI Standard	Burst Transfer
II. SCSI-1	5 MB/s
III. SCSI-2 (Fast SCSI, Fast Narrow)	10 MB/s
IV. SCSI-2 Fast Wide (Wide SCSI)	20 MB/s
V. SCSI-2 Differential Narrow	10 MB/s
VI. SCSI-2 Differential Wide	20 MB/s
VII. SCSI-3 Ultra Narrow (Fast-20)	20 MB/s
VIII. SCSI-3 Ultra Wide	40 MB/s
IX. SCSI-3 Wide Ultra2	80 MB/s

X. SCSI-3 Wide Ultra3	320 MB/s

As an it auditor what you know about SHARE RECOVERY TIERS

A. Tier 0: No off-site data – Possibly no recovery
B. Tier 1: Data backup with no hot site
C. Tier 2: Data backup with a hot site
D. Tier 3: Electronic vaulting
E. Tier 4: Point-in-time copies
F. Tier 5: Transaction integrity
G. Tier 6: Zero or near-Zero data loss
H. Tier 7: Highly automated, business integrated solution

Rebuild time of failed drive=Equalization Rate= Speed at which the hot spare is copied to replacement for a failed disk.

Time = ((Failed Hard Drive Capacity * Rebuild Rate) * Disk Type and Speed Adjustment) + (Failed Hard Drive Capacity * Equalization Rate)

As an it auditor what you know about RAID SPECIFICATIONS

RAID levels 3, 4, and 5 use the N+1 formula

Where the capacity of N number of devices will be used for data and the capacity of one of those devices will be dedicated to data protection, or Parity.

Usable + Parity = Raw Capacity

A. Raid 0 (Stripe): Minimum 2 disks, Excellent performance ,No redundancy

B. Raid 1 (Mirror): 2 Drives, High performance, High redundancy, very minimal penalty on write performance.

C. Raid 5 (Drives with Parity): Minimum 3 Drives, Good performance, Good redundancy, Good Price.

D. Raid 6 (Drives with Double Parity): Minimum 4 Drives, Additional fault tolerance.

E. Raid 10 (Mirror+Stripe) or 0+1 (Stripe+Mirror): Minimum 4 Drives, Stripe of mirrors, excellent redundancy, excellent performance. Usable capacity 50% of available disk drives

F. Raid 50 (Parity+Stripe): Minimum 6 Drives. Usable capacity is between 67% - 94%, fast, data redundancy.

G. Raid 60 (Double Parity+Stripe): Minimum 8 Drives, Usable capacity 50% - 88%, fast, extra data redundancy.

As an it auditor what you know about LUN ID

A SCSI address consists of a Target ID and a Logical Unit Number (LUN).
LUN ID is in hexadecimal value (00 - FF), which is mapped to the specified volume ID, Using a Decimal to hex converter, convert decimal number to hexadecimal as:

Device Address=the hexadecimal value that uniquely defines a physical I/O device on a channel path.

Decimal	Hex	Binary	Value
A. 000	00	00000000	
B. 001	01	00000001	
C. 002	02	00000010	
D. 003	03	00000011	
E. 004	04	00000100	
F. 005	05	00000101	
G. 006	06	00000110	
H. 007	07	00000111	
I. 008	08	00001000	

J. 009	09	00001001
K. 010	0A	00001010
L. 011	0B	00001011
M. 012	0C	00001100
N. 013	0D	00001101
O. 014	0E	00001110
P. 015	0F	00001111
Q. 016	10	00010000
R. 017	11	00010001
S. 018	12	00010010
T. 019	13	00010011
U. 020	14	00010100

As an it auditor what you know about HDD RELIABILITY

I. MTTF = Mean Time to Failure
II. MTTR = Mean Time to Repair
III. MTBF = Mean Time between Failures = MTTF + MTTR
IV. MTBF = (Total Time of all Parts run) / (Total number of failures)

As an it auditor what you know about SUPPORTED DISTANCES OF THE VARIOUS 62.5-MICRON CABLES

Speed	Length
1.0625 Gb	2 m (6.6 ft) min to 300 m (985 ft) max
2.125 Gb	2 m (6.6 ft) min to 150 m (492 ft) max
4 Gb	2 m (6.6 ft) min to 70 m (231 ft) max

As an it auditor what you know about BUFFER TO BUFFER CREDITS FOR LONG DISTANCE

A good rule of thumb is to use 1 BB credit for each kilometer (km) multiplied by the speed of the FC connection.

A. 1 Gigabit	0.5 Credit Per Kilometer
B. 2 Gigabit	1 Credit Per Kilometer

As an it auditor what you know about AVAILABILITY

System Availability: Availability = Uptime/ (Uptime + Downtime)

Availability Downtime
- A. 99%   3.65 days a year.
- B. 99.9% 8.76 hours a year.
- C. 99.99%   52.56 minutes a year.
- D. 99.999%   5.26 minutes a year.

As an it auditor what you know about LATENCY AND RPM

Latency time = (1/((Rotational Speed in RPM)/60)) * 0.5 * 1000 mili seconds

HDD Spindle RPM	Average rotational latency [ms]
I. 7,200	4.17
II. 10,000	3.00
III. 15,000	2.00

As an it auditor what you know about SAS

6Gb/s SAS, Double transfer rate to 6Gb/s, Up to 10m cable lengths

As an it auditor what you know about RETURN ON INVESTMENT (ROI)

ROI = (Net Profit / Cost of Investment) x 100
Total Cost of Ownership (TCO): It incorporates hardware and software costs, installation and license tracking, warranties and maintenance agreements.

As an it auditor what you know about RECOVERY

RPO= Maximum tolerable data loss (time since last backup)
RTO=Time needed from failure to recover and resume to business

The required Bandwidth=the required bandwidth is determined by measuring the average number of write operations and the average size of write operations over a period of time.

As an it auditor what you know about MODE CONDITIONING FIBER OPTIC CABLE

SUPPORTED DISTANCES OF THE VARIOUS 50-MICRON CABLES:

	Data rate/Link speed	M5 (OM2) cable	M5E (OM3) cable	M5F (OM4) cable
1	8 Gbps	50 m (164 ft.)	150 m (492 ft.)	190 m (623 ft.)
2	4 Gbps	150 m (492 ft.)	380 m (1 247 ft.)	400 m (1312 ft.)

As an it auditor what you know about Data-at-Rest encryption

Triple DES uses a "key bundle" which comprises three DES keys, K1, K2 and K3, each of 56 bits (excluding parity bits). The encryption algorithm is:

ciphertext = EK3(DK2(EK1(plaintext)))

Each triple encryption encrypts one block of 64 bits of data.

As an it auditor what you know about Linux operating systems commands?

- ❖ pwd Print the working directory.
- ❖ Hostname Find my computer name.
- ❖ Cd Change the directory.
- ❖ Ls List the contents of a directory.
- ❖ Ls Find the contents of the directory you are currently in.
- ❖ Rmdir Delete the directory.
- ❖ Mv Rename a file.
- ❖ Cp Copy a file.
- ❖ Cat Print the whole file.
- ❖ Find Find files.
- ❖ Grep Find things inside files.
- ❖ Man Find the manual.
- ❖ Chmod Change the permission modifier.
- ❖ Chown Change ownership.
- ❖ touch Create a blank file
- ❖ top Display a continually updating report of system resource usage.
- ❖ Iostat Current CPU load average and disk I/O information.

❖ ps –ef Processes currently running.

As an it auditor what you know about WI-FI SECURITY

WPA2 encryption

WPA2-PSK (Preshared Key) is the strongest and most practical form of WPA for most home users. WPA2 is more secure than WPA because it uses the much stronger AES (Advanced Encryption Standard) protocol for encrypting packets

I.   WPA2

Wi-Fi Protected Access 2
Introduced September 2004
Two Versions
Enterprise – Server Authentication 802.1x
Personal – AES Pre-Shared Key
Full implementation of 802.11i

II.   WPA2-PSK

Pre-Shared Key Mode
Network traffic encrypted using a 256 bit PMK

User enters key (Pairwise Master Key)
64 hex digits
8-63 Printable ASCII characters
Takes the passphrase, SSID of AP, 4096 iterations of HMAC-SHA-1

As an it auditor what you know about BOTNET

I.   Botnet is a computer infection that allows several computers to launch attacks against a network.
II.   It's a Network of autonomous programs capable of acting on instructions.
III.   An IRC based, command and control network of compromised hosts (bots)
IV.   A bot is a client program that runs in the background of a compromised host
V.   It watches for certain strings on an IRC channel
VI.   These are encoded commands for the bot
VII.   It's used by hackers for DoS, ID Theft, Phishing, key logging, spam

As an it auditor what you know about MALWARE

I.   Viruses: require the spreading of an infected host file
II.   Worms: standalone software, file-transport, a worm self-replicates but a virus can not.
III.   Trojans: tricked into loading and executing on systems
IV.   Bots: automate tasks and provide services
V.   Spyware: is a malware that captures personal information
VI.   Adware, any software that covertly gathers user information

As an it auditor what you know about IP ADDRESS CLASSES

I.   Class A: 0-127
II.   Class B: 128 - 191
III. Class C: 192-223
IV.   Class D: 224-238
V.   Class E: 239-255

Class A   A Class A address uses only the first octet to represent the network portion

1 to 126
126 Networks
16,777,214 hosts

Class B   A Class B address uses two octets to represent the network portion

128 to 191

Networks 16,384

65,534 hosts per network

Class C   A Class C address uses three octets to represent the network portion

192 to 223.255.255.255

Networks 2,097,152

Class D   Class D is reserved for multicast addressing

224 to 239.x.x.x

Class E   Class E is reserved for future development

240 to 255.x.x.x

As an it auditor what you know about MAC ADDRESS FORMAT

I.   A MAC address is also called a physical address because it is physically embedded in the interface.

II.   A MAC address is a 6-byte (48-bit) hexadecimal address that enables a NIC to be uniquely identified on the network.

III.   The MAC address forms the basis of network communication, regardless of the protocol used to achieve network connection.

IV.   MAC addresses are expressed in hexadecimal, only the numbers 0 through 9 and the letters A through F can be used in them.

As an it auditor what you know about MULTICAST

I.   Multicasting is a mechanism by which groups of network devices can send and receive data between the members of the group at one time, instead of separately sending messages to each device in the group.

II.   The multicast grouping is established by configuring each device with the same multicast IP address.

As an it auditor what you know about UNICAST

I.   With a unicast address, a single address is specified.
II.   Data sent with unicast addressing is delivered to a specific node identified by the address.
III.   It is a point-to-point address link.

As an it auditor what you know about BROADCAST

A broadcast address is at the opposite end of the spectrum from a unicast address.

A broadcast address is an IP address that you can use to target all systems on a subnet or network instead of single hosts. In other words, a broadcast message goes to everyone on the network.

As an it auditor what you know about IPV6

I.   IPv6 uses a 128-bit addressing scheme.

II.   An IPv6 address is divided along 16-bit boundaries, and each
16-bit block is converted into a four-digit hexadecimal number and separated by colons.

III.   IPv6 address has eight fields and each field contains four hexadecimal digits.

IV.   IPv6 address is a 128-bit address: 4 bits per digit * 4 digits per field * 8 fields = 128 bits in an IPv6 address

As an it auditor what you know about loop back address

IPv4 reserves 127.0.0.1 as the loopback address. IPv6 has the same reservation.

As an it auditor what you know about the standard ports

#	PORT	SERVICES
1	25	SMTP
2	22	SSH
3	110	POP3
4	80	HTTP
5	123	NTP
6	220	IMAP3
7	119	NNTP
8	115	SFTP
9	3389	REMOTE DESKTOP
10	443	SSL
11	23	TELNET
12	69	TFTP

13	143	IMAP
14	443	HTTPS
15	20/21	FTP
16	53	DNS
17	161	SNMP
18	546	DHCP CLIENT
19	389	LDAP
20	137	NETBIOS

As an IT auditor what you know about TRACERT

I.   The TRACERT (Trace Route) command is a route-tracing utility used to determine the path that an IP packet has taken to reach a destination.

II.   The TRACERT diagnostic utility determines the route taken to a destination by sending Internet Control Message Protocol (ICMP) echo packets with varying IP Time-To-Live (TTL) values to the destination.

III.   Note you can run this utility by typing tracert IPAddress or tracert HostName at the command prompt.

IV.   Tracert is used to list all of the hops from a starting point

As an IT auditor what you know about DSL

I.   Digital subscriber line (DSL, originally digital subscriber loop) is a family of technologies that provide Internet access by transmitting digital data over the wires of a local telephone network.

II.   The bit rate of consumer DSL services typically ranges from 256 kbit/s to 40 Mbit/s in the direction to the customer (downstream), depending on DSL technology, line conditions, and service-level implementation

Non Technical/Personal/HR Interview: Complimentary

Bottom Line Job interview?

Bottom-line: You will learn to answer any questions in such a way that you match your qualifications to the job requirements.

Interview Question?

Example response. Try to customize your answers to fit the requirements of the job you are interviewing for.

What are your greatest strengths?

I. **Articulate.**
II. **Achiever.**
III. **Organized.**
IV. **Intelligence.**
V. **Honesty.**
VI. **Team Player.**
VII. **Perfectionist.**
VIII. **Willingness.**
IX. **Enthusiasm.**
X. **Motivation.**
XI. **Confident.**
XII. **Healthy.**
XIII. **Likeability.**
XIV. **Positive Attitude.**
XV. **Sense of Humor.**
XVI. **Good Communication Skills.**
XVII. **Dedication.**
XVIII. **Constructive Criticism.**
XIX. **Honesty.**
XX. **Very Consistent.**
XXI. **Determination.**
XXII. **Ability to Get Things Done.**
XXIII. **Analytical Abilities.**
XXIV. **Problem Solving Skills.**

XXV. Flexibility.
XXVI. Active in the Professional Societies.
XXVII. Prioritize.
XXVIII. Gain Knowledge by Reading Journals.
XXIX. Attention to details.
XXX. Vendor management skills.
XXXI. Excellent Project Management skills.
XXXII. Self-disciplined.
XXXIII. Self-reliant.
XXXIV. Self-starter.
XXXV. Leadership.
XXXVI. Team-building.
XXXVII. Multitasking.
XXXVIII. Prioritization.
XXXIX. Time management.
XL. Can handle multiple projects and deadlines.
XLI. Thrives under pressure.
XLII. A great motivator.
XLIII. An amazing problem solver.
XLIV. Someone with extraordinary attention to detail.
XLV. Confident.
XLVI. Assertive.
XLVII. Persistent.
XLVIII. Reliable.
XLIX. Understand people.
L. Handle multiple priorities.
LI. Build rapport with strangers.

What are your greatest weaknesses?

I. I am working on My Management skills.
II. I feel I could do things on my own in a faster way without delegating it.
III. Currently I am learning to delegate work to staff members.
IV. I have a sense of urgency and I tend to push people to get work done.
V. I focus on details and think thru the process start to finish and sometimes miss out the overall picture, so I am improving my skills by laying a schedule to monitor overall progress.

Had you failed to do any work and regret?

     I. **I have No Regrets.**
     II. **I am Moving on.**

Where do you see yourself five years from now?

     I. **I am looking for a long-term commitment.**
     II. **I see a great chance to perform and grow with the company.**
     III. **I will continue to learn and take on additional responsibilities.**
     IV. **If selected I will continue rise to any challenge, pursue all tasks to completion, and accomplish all goals in a timely manner.**
     V. **I am sure if I will continue to do my work and achieve results more and more opportunities will open up for me.**
     VI. **I will try to take the path of progression, and hope to progress upwards.**
     VII. **In the long run I would like to move on from a technical position to a management position where I am able to smoothly manage, delegate and accomplish goals on time.**
     VIII. **I want to Mentor and lead junior-to-mid level reporting analysts.**
     IX. **I want to enhance my management experience in motivating and building strong teams.**
     X. **I want to build and manage relationships at all levels in the organization.**
     XI. **I want to get higher degree, new certification.**

How Will You Achieve Your Goals?

Advancing skills by taking related classes, professional associations, participating in conferences, attending seminars, continuing my education.

Why are you leaving Your Current position?

I. More money
II. Opportunity
III. Responsibility
IV. Growth
V. Downsizing and upcoming merger, so I made a good, upward career move before my department came under the axe of the new owners.

Why are you looking for a new job?

I have been promoted as far as I can go with my   current employer.
I'm looking for a new challenge that will give me the opportunity to use my skills to help me grow with the company.

Why should I hire you?

I. **I know this business from ground up.**
II. **I have Strong background in this Skill.**
III. **Proven, solid experience and track record.**
IV. **Highest level of commitment.**
V. **Continuous education on current technical issues.**
VI. **Direct experience in leading.**
VII. **Hands-on experience.**
VIII. **Excellent Project Management skills.**
IX. **Demonstrated achievements.**
X. **Knowledge base.**
XI. **Communications skills.**
XII. **Ability to analyze, diagnoses, suggests, and implements process changes.**
XIII. **Strong customer service orientation.**
XIV. **Detail oriented, strong analytical, organizational, and problem solving skill.**
XV. **Ability to interact with all levels.**
XVI. **Strong interpersonal, relationship management skills.**
XVII. **Ability to work effectively with all levels, cultures, functions.**
XVIII. **I am a good team player.**
XIX. **Extensive Technical experience.**
XX. **Understanding of Business.**

XXI. Result and customer-oriented.
XXII. Strong communication skills.
XXIII. Good Project and Resource management skills.
XXIV. Exceptional interpersonal and customer service skills.
XXV. Strong analytical, evaluative, problem-solving abilities.
XXVI. Good management and planning skills.
XXVII. Good Time Management skills.
XXVIII. Ability to work independently.
XXIX. I've been very carefully looking for the jobs.
XXX. I can bring XX years of experience.
XXXI. That, along with my flexibility and organizational skills, makes me a perfect match for this position.
XXXII. I see some challenges ahead of me here, and that's what I thrive on.
XXXIII. I have all the qualifications that you need, and you have an opportunity that I want. It's a 100% Fit.

Aren' t you overqualified for this position?

I. In My opinion in the current economy and the volatile job market overqualified is a relative term.
II. My experience and qualifications make me do the job right.
III. I am interested in a long term relationship with my employer.
IV. As you can see my skills match perfectly.
V. Please see my longevity with previous employers.
VI. I am the perfect candidate for the position.
VII. What else can I do to convince you that I am the best candidate? There will be positive benefits due to this. Since I have strong experience in this ABC skill I will start to contribute quickly. I have all the training and experience needed to do this job. There's just no substitute for hands on experience.

Describe a Typical Work Week?

I. Meeting every morning to evaluate current issues.
II. Check emails, voice messages.
III. Project team meeting.
IV. Prioritize issues.

V. Design, configure, implement, maintain, and support. Perform architectural design. Review and analysis of business reports.
VI. Conduct weekly staff meetings.
VII. Support of strategic business initiatives.
VIII. Any duties as assigned. Implementation.
IX. Monitor and analyze reports. Routine maintenance and upgrades.
X. Technical support.
XI. Deploy and maintain.
XII. Provide day-to-day support as required. Work with customers and clients.
XIII. Documentation.
XIV. Standard operating procedures.
XV. Tactical planning.
XVI. Determine and recommend.
XVII. Plan and coordinate the evaluation.
XVIII. Effective implementation of technology solutions.
XIX. To meet the business objectives.
XX. Participation in budget matters.
XXI. Readings to Keep Abreast Of Current Trends and Developments in the Field.

Are You Willing to Travel?

I. For the right opportunity I am open to travel.
II. I'm open to opportunities so if it involves relocation I would consider it.

Describe the pace at which you work?

I. I work at a consistent and steady pace.
II. I try to complete work in advance of the deadline.
III. I am able to manage multiple projects simultaneously.
IV. I am flexible with my work speed and try to conclude my projects on time.
V. So far I have achieved all my targets
VI. I meet or exceeded my goals.

How Did You Handle Challenges?

I. Whenever the project got out of track I managed to get the project schedules back on the track.
II. Whenever there was an issue I had researched the issues and found the solutions.
III. We were able to successfully troubleshoot the issues and solve the problems, within a very short period of time.

How do you handle pressure? Stressful situations?

I. In personal life I manage stress by going to a health club.
II. I remain calm in crisis.
III. I can work calmly with many supervisors at the same time.
IV. I use the work stress and pressure in a constructive manner.
V. I use pressure to stay focused, motivated and productive.
VI. I like working in a challenging environment.
VII. By Prioritizing.
VIII. Use time management
IX. Use problem-solving
X. Use decision-making skills to reduce stress.
XI. Making a "to-do" list.
XII. Site stress-reducing techniques such as stretching and taking a break.
XIII. Asked for assistance when overwhelmed.

How Many Hours Do You Work?

I enjoy solving problems and work as much as necessary to get the job done.
The Norm is 40 hour week.

Why are you the best person for the job?

I. It's a perfect fit as you need someone like me who can produce results that you need, and my background and experience are proof.
II. As you can see in My resume I've held a lot of similar positions like this one, and hence I am a perfect fit as all those experiences will help me here.
III. I believe this is a good place to work and it will help me excel.

What are you looking for in a position?

I. I'm looking for an opportunity where I may be able to apply my skills and significantly contribute to the growth of the company while helping create some advancement and more opportunities for myself.
II. It seems this organization will appreciate my contributions and reward my efforts appropriately to keep me motivated.
III. I am looking for job satisfaction and the total compensation package to meet My Worth that will allow me to make enough money to support my lifestyle.

What do you know about our organization?

I. This is an exciting place to work and it fits my career goals.
II. This company has an impressive growth.
III. I think it would be rewarding to be a part of such a company.

What are your short term goals?

I'd like to find a position that is a good fit and where I can contribute and satisfy my professional desires.

What Salary are you looking for?

I. Please provide me the information about the job and the responsibilities involved before we can begin to discuss salary.
II. Please give me an idea of the range you may have budgeted for this position.
III. It seems my skills meet your highest standards so I would expect a salary at the highest end of your budget.
IV. I believe someone with my experience should get between A and B.
V. Currently I am interested in talking more about what the position can offer my career.
VI. I am flexible but, I'd like to learn more about the position and your staffing needs.
VII. I am very interested in finding the right opportunity and will be open to any fair offer you may have.

Tell me more about yourself.

I. I'm an experienced professional with extensive knowledge.
II. Information tools and techniques.
III. My Education.
IV. A prominent career change.
V. Personal and professional values.
VI. Personal data.
VII. Hobbies.
VIII. Interests.
IX. Describe each position.
X. Overall growth.
XI. Career destination.

Why did you leave your previous job?

I. Relocation.
II. Ambition for growth.
III. This new opportunity is a better fit for my skills and/or career ambitions.
IV. To advance my career and get a position that allows me to grow.
V. I was in an unfortunate situation of having been downsized.

VI.   I'm looking for a change of direction.
VII. I want to visit different part of the country I'm looking to relocate.
VIII. I am looking to move up with more scope for progression.

What relevant experience do you have?

I have these XYZ related experience.
I have these skills that can apply to internal management positions et al.

If your previous co-workers were here, what would they say about you?

Hard worker, most reliable, creative problem-solver, Flexible, Helping

Where else have you applied?

I am seriously looking and keeping my options open.

What motivates you to do a good job?

Recognition for a job well done.

Are you good at working in a team?

Yes.

Has anything ever irritated you about people you've worked with?

I've always got on just fine with all my co-workers.

Is there anyone you just could not work with?

No.

Tell me about any issues you' ve had with a previous boss.

I never had any issues with my boss.

Do you have any questions?

**Please explain the benefits and bonus.
How soon could I start, if I were offered the job?**

Why did you choose this career?

    **I. Life style.
   II. Passion.
  III. Desire.
  IV. Interesting.
   V. Challenging.
  VI. Pays Well.
 VII. Demand.**

What did you learn from your last job experience?

I gained experience that's directly related to this job.

Why is there a gap in your resume?

**Because of Personal and family reasons I was unable to work
for some time.
   I. Unemployed.
  II. Job hunt.
 III. Layoffs.**

How do you keep current and informed about your job and the industries that you have worked in?

I. **I pride myself on my ability to stay on top of what is happening in the industry.**
II. **I do a lot of reading.**
III. **I belong to a couple of professional organizations.**
IV. **I have a strong network with colleagues.**
V. **I take classes and seminars.**
VI. **I have started and participated in many technical blogs.**

Tell me about a time when you had to plan and coordinate a project from start to finish?

I. **I headed up a project which involved customer service personnel and technicians.**
II. **I organized a meeting and got everyone together.**
III. **I drew up a plan, using all best of the ideas.**
IV. **I organized teams.**
V. **We had a deadline to meet, so I did periodic checks with various teams involved.**
VI. **After four weeks, we were exceeding expectations.**
VII. **We were able to begin implementation of the plan.**
VIII. **It was a great team effort, and a big success.**
IX. **I was commended by management for my managing capacity.**

What kinds of people do you have difficulties working with?

I. **I have worked in very diverse teams.**
II. **Diversity means differences and similarities with men and women from very diverse backgrounds and culture. It helps us grow as a human being.**
III. **The only difficulty was related to work related dishonesty by a person.**
IV. **He was taking credit for all the work our team accomplished.**

What do you want to be in 5 years?

I hope to develop my management skills by managing a small staff.

Explain an Ideal career for you?

    I.   **I would like to stay in a field of ABC.**
    II. **I have been good at ABC.**
    III. **I look forward to ABC.**

What are your job responsibilities?

I would expect expanded responsibilities that could make use of my other skills.

What is your dream job?

Includes all of the responsibilities and duties you are trying to fill.
I also thrive in the fast changing environment where there is business growth.

What skills you have?

I was very pleased to develop the A, B, C skills that you are seeking.

What sets you apart?

    I.   **Once I am committed to a job or project I take it with tremendous intensity.**
    II. **I want to learn everything I can.**

III. **I am very competitive and like to excel at everything I do.**

If the project not gone as planned what action you will take?

Backup and identify precautions.

What you do if you are unable to meet deadlines?

I. **Negotiate.**
II. **Discussion.**
III. **Restructure.**
IV. **Redefine Optimum goal.**
V. **Show a price structure.**

Interpersonal skill?

I. **I had to learn to say no.**
II. **Helpful to other staff.**
III. **Help in return.**

Improve?

In any job I hold I can usually find inefficiencies in a process, come up with a solution.

What do you feel has been your greatest work-related

accomplishment?

I. **Implemented an idea to reduce expenses, raised revenues.**
II. **Solved real problems.**
III. **Enhanced department's reputation.**

Have you ever had to discipline a problem employee? If so, how did you handle it?

Yes.

I did it using:

    I. **Problem-solving skills**
    II. **Listening skills, and**
    III. **Coaching skills**

Why do you want this position?

    I. **I always wanted the opportunity to work with a company that leads the industry in innovative products.**
    II. **My qualifications and goals complement the company's mission, vision and values.**
    III. **I will be able to apply and expand on the knowledge and experience, and will be able to increase my contributions and value to the company through new responsibilities.**

Why are you the best person for this job?

    I. **I have extensive experience in XYZ (Skill they are looking for)**
    II. **I'm a fast learner.**
    III. **I adapt quickly to change.**
    IV. **I will hit the ground running.**
    V. **I'm dedicated and enthusiastic.**
    VI. **I'm an outstanding performer.**
    VII. **I may be lacking in this specific experience but I'm a fast learner and I'll work harder.**

What about Technical writing?

I. I can convert any complex technical information into simple, easy form.

II. I can write reports to achieve maximum results.

How versatile you are? Can you do other works?

I am flexible and can adapt to any changing situations.

How do you manage time?

I. I am very process oriented and I use a systematic approach to achieve more in very less time.

II. I effectively eliminate much paperwork.

How do you handle Conflicts?

I. I am very tactful;
II. I avoid arguments and frictions and
III. I establish trust and mutual understanding.

What kind of supervisory skills you have?

I. I make sure that everyone understands their responsibilities.
II. I try to be realistic in setting the expectations and try to balance the work among all.

Any Bad Situation you could not solve?

I've never yet come across any situation that couldn't be resolved by a determined, constructive effort.

Anything else you want to say?

I. I am excited and enthusiastic about this opportunity
II. I am looking forward to working with you.

Author/Publisher Information

About the author:

/editor/compiler:
Kumar is an author, educator, and an IT professional and he
enjoys sharing his expertise on wide variety of subjects in easy
language to help all his readers.
Publisher: BOTTOM LINE GS LLC

The course material is copyrighted and for your use exclusively.
It should not be shared with anyone else.

www.ingramcontent.com/pod-product-compliance
Lightning Source LLC
LaVergne TN
LVHW022304060326
832902LV00020B/3270